The WordPress User Guide For Beginners 2025

Tips and Tricks for Maximizing Performance, Productivity, and Unlock Your Creative Potential

Ray V. Lopez

Copyright © 2025 by Ray V. Lopez.

All rights reserved.

No part of this book may be reproduced, distributed, or transmitted in any form or by any means, including photocopying, recording, or other electronic or mechanical methods, without the prior written permission of the publisher, except in the case of brief quotations embodied in critical reviews and certain other noncommercial uses permitted by copyright law.

Contents

Introduction..6
   How to Use This Guide...6
   The WordPress in 2025..7

Chapter 1...10
Getting Started On The WordPress and Website Building..................................10
   What is WordPress? Understanding CMS and Its Power....................................10
   Difference Between WordPress.com and WordPress.org.....................................11
   Why Choose WordPress in 2025? Latest Trends and Benefits............................12
   Types of Websites You Can Build with WordPress..15
   Overview of the WordPress Ecosystem...18
   Key Terminologies Every Beginner Must Know..20
   Setting Realistic Expectations: What You Can Achieve as a Beginner...............24

Chapter 2...26
Planning Your Website — Strategy Before Setup...26
   Defining Your Website's Purpose and Goals..26
   Choosing the Right Domain Name and Brand Identity.......................................28
   Understanding Your Target Audience..30
   Planning Website Structure: Pages, Posts, Categories, and Menus....................31
   Creating a Content Strategy: What to Publish and When...................................33
   Wireframing Your Site Layout: Tools and Techniques for Beginners................35
   Checklist: Preparing for a Successful WordPress Launch..................................37

Chapter 3...42
Setting Up Your WordPress Site from Scratch...42
   Choosing the Best Hosting Provider for Your Needs..42
   Step-by-Step Domain Registration and DNS Setup..45
   Troubleshooting Common Domain Issues..46
   One-Click WordPress Installation vs Manual Installation..................................47
   Exploring the WordPress Dashboard: First Look and Overview........................49
   Essential Settings: General, Permalinks, Reading, and Discussion....................51
   Understanding WordPress User Roles and Permissions.....................................53
   Security Best Practices from Day One: Passwords, SSL, and Backups.............55

Chapter 4...58
Mastering the WordPress Block Editor (Gutenberg)...58
   Introduction to the Block Editor Interface..58
   Using Basic Blocks: Paragraph, Heading, Image, Lists, Quotes.........................60

    Advanced Blocks: Unlocking Creative Flexibility... 63
    Creating Beautiful Pages and Posts with Layouts and Design Tips.. 66
    Reusable Blocks and Templates: Saving Time and Ensuring Consistency............................. 68
    Troubleshooting Common Block Editor Issues... 69
    Alternatives and Page Builders: When and Why to Use Them... 71

Chapter 5.... **74**

Selecting and Customizing Themes Like a Pro... **74**
    Understanding WordPress Themes: Free vs Premium.. 74
    How to Choose a Fast, SEO-Friendly, and Responsive Theme... 76
    Customizing Your Theme Like a Pro... 77
    Installing and Activating Themes: Step-by-Step.. 79
    Using the WordPress Customizer: Colors, Fonts, Layouts, and More................................... 80
    Child Themes: Why They Matter and How to Create One.. 82
    Popular Theme Recommendations for Different Website Types in 2025............................... 83
    Fixing Common Theme Issues and Compatibility Tips... 85

Chapter 6.... **88**

Essential Plugins for Every Website... **88**
    What Are Plugins and Why They Matter... 88
    How to Find, Install, and Activate Plugins Safely... 89
    Must-Have Plugins for Every Website... 91
    Must-Have Plugins for SEO, Security, Speed, and Backups... 92
    Plugins for Enhancing User Experience: Contact Forms, Social Sharing, Analytics............. 95
    Avoiding Plugin Conflicts and Performance Issues.. 96
    Step-by-Step Guide to Building Custom Functionality Without Coding................................ 98

Chapter 7.... **102**

Creating and Managing Content Effectively... **102**
    The Difference Between Posts and Pages — When to Use Each... 102
    Organizing Content with Categories and Tags... 103
    Creating and Managing Posts and Pages... 104
    Best Practices for Writing SEO-Friendly Content in 2025.. 105
    Adding Images, Videos, and Other Media Correctly... 107
    Using Galleries, Sliders, and Featured Images.. 108
    Scheduling Posts and Managing Content Calendar... 109
    Editing and Updating Content Without Breaking Your Site.. 111

Chapter 8.... **114**

Website Navigation and User Experience (UX)... **114**
    Designing Clear Menus and Navigation Structures... 114
    Creating Footer and Sidebar Widgets.. 116

- Optimizing Your Site for Mobile Visitors..118
- Accessibility Basics: Making Your Site Inclusive...119
- Adding Search Functionality and Breadcrumbs..121
- Speed Optimization Techniques: Caching, Image Compression, and Lazy Loading............122
- Testing UX: Tools and Techniques to Improve Visitor Interaction................................124

Chapter 9..128
Securing Your WordPress Site and Managing Backups..................................128
- Understanding WordPress Security Risks and Vulnerabilities......................................128
- Implementing Strong Password Policies..130
- Protecting Your Website with Firewalls and Anti-Malware Plugins.................................133
- Configuring Regular Backups: Manual and Automated Methods..................................136
- Restoring Your Site from Backups: Step-by-Step Guide..139
- Managing User Access and Monitoring Site Activity...141

Chapter 10..146
SEO and Analytics for WordPress Beginners..146
- What Is SEO?...146
- Installing and Configuring SEO Plugins...147
- Optimizing Titles for Maximum Impact..151
- Crafting Effective Meta Descriptions..152
- Using Sitemaps Effectively..153
- Setting Up Website Analytics for Your WordPress Site..156
- Key Metrics to Track and What They Mean...156
- Interpreting Traffic Data to Improve Your Site..157
- Tips to Improve Your Rankings in 2025's Search Landscape......................................158

Chapter 11..160
Monetizing Your WordPress Website..160
- Overview of Monetization Options for WordPress..160
- Setting Up an Online Store with WooCommerce...162
- Unlocking Recurring Revenue: Using Membership and Subscription Plugins...................165
- Creating and Selling Online Courses or Digital Downloads...167
- Integrating Payment Gateways Securely...169
- Email Marketing and List Building with WordPress..170
- Legal Considerations: Privacy Policy, GDPR Compliance, and Terms of Service...............171

Chapter 12..174
Maintaining and Growing Your WordPress Site..174
- Regular Maintenance Tasks: Updates, Cleanup, and Performance Checks.....................174
- Using Staging Sites for Safe Testing and Updates...176
- Handling Comments and Community Management..178

Leveraging Social Media Integration...179
Scaling Your Site: From Hobby to Business.. 180
Resources for Continuous Learning: Forums, Tutorials, and WordPress Events.................. 181
Final Checklist and Troubleshooting Guide for Beginners.. 183
Conclusion.. **186**

Introduction

This statistic conveys a compelling narrative: WordPress has evolved from a basic blogging platform to the foundation of numerous personal blogs, commercial websites, e-commerce platforms, portfolios, and prominent news organizations.

Regardless of whether you aim to initiate your inaugural blog, create an impressive portfolio, or establish an online enterprise, WordPress provides the versatility and resources necessary to achieve these objectives—without requiring development expertise or technical proficiency.

Who This Guide Is For:

This book is developed just for you — the newbie who may feel overwhelmed by the world of website construction but is determined to produce a professional, functional, and attractive site using WordPress. You may have experimented with alternative platforms and discovered them to be overly complex or limiting.

You may have heard that WordPress is the most popular website builder, but you are uncertain about how to begin. Or, you might simply wish to learn how to run your own website confidently, without relying on pricey developers or agencies.

If any of these descriptors sound like you, then this guide is the perfect companion for your adventure.

No prior expertise in coding, web design, or advanced computer abilities beyond the basics is required. A willingness to learn and adherence to explicit instructions are all that is required.

This guide employs clear language, thoroughly elucidating each phase, bolstered by authentic examples and pragmatic counsel. Our objective is to empower you with the knowledge and abilities to construct and manage your own WordPress site from the start.

How to Use This Guide

One of the most crucial things when learning something new is having the correct attitude and materials. This book is structured to help you proceed seamlessly from knowing the basics to developing critical abilities. Here's how to make the most of it:

- **Step-by-Step Instructions:** Each chapter breaks down complex tasks into simple, manageable steps. Follow along carefully, and don't rush ahead. WordPress offers many options, and knowing when and how to use them will save you time and frustration.

- **Hands-On Learning:** This is not just theory. Throughout the guide, you'll be encouraged to try things yourself — whether it's installing WordPress, choosing a theme, or adding content. The more you practice, the faster you'll become confident.

- **Visual Aids and Examples:** Though this is a written guide, references to screenshots, diagrams, and examples will help you understand each concept. If you prefer, you can complement this book with online video tutorials or WordPress forums, but everything you need to start is here.

- **Troubleshooting Tips:** Websites don't always behave as expected. We'll provide common issues and solutions so you can handle hiccups without panic.

- **Flexible Reading:** Feel free to read the chapters in order or jump to sections that interest you most. However, the chapters build on each other, so reading sequentially is recommended for the best experience.

- **Supplementary Resources:** At the end of the book, you'll find additional tips, a glossary of terms, and resources to help you grow your site beyond the basics.

The WordPress in 2025

Before you plunge into designing your site, it's vital to understand what WordPress really is and why it continues to rule the web.

WordPress began in 2003 as a blogging platform but has now expanded into a full content management system (CMS). This means it allows you to write, modify, organize, and publish any kinds of material on the web – from blog articles to product listings and beyond. Its strength comes in its flexibility, ease of use, and enormous community that offers themes, plugins, and support.

WordPress is free to use, but to make your website live on the internet, you'll need two things: a domain name (your website's address) and hosting (a place where your website files are stored). The choices you make here will affect your website's performance, security, and growth potential.

This guide will follow you through every step – from registering your domain to installing WordPress, selecting the proper theme, customizing your site's look and functionality, and posting your first content.

In 2025, WordPress is stronger than ever, with new tools and upgrades meant to make site-building more accessible, faster, and enjoyable:

- The **Block Editor** (Gutenberg) provides a visual way to design pages using blocks of text, images, buttons, and more.

- Improved **Site Health** tools help you monitor your website's performance and security.

- Expanded **Theme and Plugin Libraries** give you thousands of options to customize your site without coding.

- Better **Mobile Optimization** ensures your site looks great on phones and tablets, where most visitors now browse.

- Enhanced **Security Features** help protect your website from hacks and malware.

This guide embraces these modern features and will help you understand how to use them to your advantage.

Building a website may seem like a daunting undertaking at first. But with the correct advice and a clear plan, it becomes an exciting project you can manage on your own. Your website will be a platform where your ideas, business, or passion may reach the globe.

As you move through this book, you'll develop skills that go beyond just WordPress. You'll learn how websites function, how to keep them safe, and how to interact with your audience. These are crucial abilities in today's digital environment.

Thank You For Choosing This Guide To Start Your Adventure. Let's Get Your Wordpress Site Up And Running, Step By Step, And Unleash The Potential That The Internet Has For You.

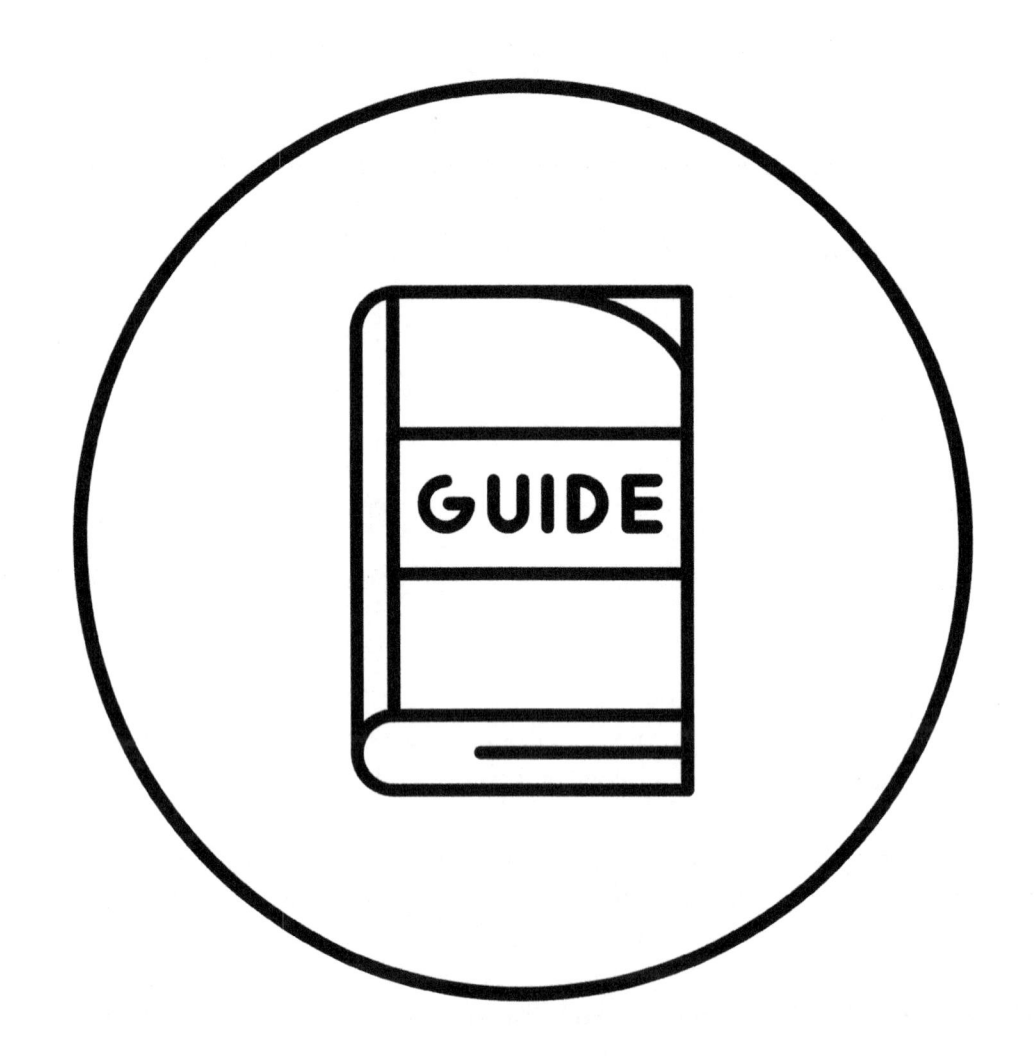

Chapter 1

Getting Started On The WordPress and Website Building

Did you know that as of 2025, WordPress runs nearly 43% of all websites worldwide? That means roughly half of the websites you visit every day, whether for shopping, reading news, or learning new skills, are developed using WordPress. This amazing reach demonstrates how WordPress has developed from a humble blogging tool into the most popular and powerful platform for constructing websites around the globe. Its success resides not merely in its widespread use but in its unrivaled flexibility, convenience of use, and ever-growing community support.

Whether you are an entrepreneur seeking to develop an online presence, a creative professional presenting your portfolio, or someone looking to share your voice with the world through a blog, WordPress offers a platform adapted to your needs. But before you start developing your site, it is vital to grasp what WordPress truly is, how it operates, and why it stands out in 2025's busy digital scene.

What is WordPress? Understanding CMS and Its Power

At its foundation, WordPress is a content management system (CMS). But what precisely does that mean?

A content management system is software that allows you to create, manage, and alter material on a website without needing to know how to code. Before CMS platforms like WordPress became widespread, making a website required knowledge of HTML, CSS, JavaScript, and other programming languages. Even making minor updates or adjustments requires technical knowledge or the assistance of a developer.

WordPress altered the game by providing an easy-to-use interface where you can add pages, compose blog entries, upload photos, and manage everything visually. Think of it as a digital workspace where your ideas and information come together in an organized, structured way that translates into a live website accessible by anybody around the world.

But WordPress is much more than just a tool to post articles. Its framework permits themes and plugins—extensions that change the style and functionality of your site. Themes decide how your website looks, while plugins offer functions like contact forms, online storefronts, search engine optimization (SEO), and more. This modular design means you can develop anything from a simple blog to a fully fledged e-commerce platform without touching a single line of code.

The essential power of WordPress comes in this blend of simplicity and adaptability. Beginners can start with basic features and build their expertise as their website expands. Meanwhile, developers can go deep into customisation and create more intricate websites utilizing the same core.

Difference Between WordPress.com and WordPress.org

One of the first barriers many novices experience is knowing the difference between WordPress.com and WordPress.org. While they share the WordPress brand and comparable interfaces, they serve entirely distinct purposes and offer various levels of customization.

WordPress.com: A Hosted Platform

WordPress.com is a commercial service run by Automattic, a firm created by one of WordPress's co-creators. It offers a hosted version of WordPress, which means you don't have to bother about finding a web host or handling server settings. You simply sign up, choose a plan (there is a free tier with limitations), and start constructing your website online.

Because WordPress.com covers hosting, security, backups, and software upgrades for you, it's an enticing alternative for newbies who wish to avoid technical maintenance. However, it comes with trade-offs:

- **Limited Customization:** Free and lower-tier plans restrict the themes and plugins you can use. You're mostly confined to what WordPress.com provides.

- **Monetization Restrictions:** Running ads or selling products requires upgrading to higher plans.

- **Less Control Over Data:** Since WordPress.com hosts your site, you don't have full access to the backend files or database.

This setup can be ideal for bloggers or hobbyists who want a simple, no-fuss website with minimal setup.

WordPress.org: The Self-Hosted Solution

WordPress.org refers to the open-source WordPress software that you can download and install on your own web hosting service. This option is often called "self-hosted WordPress" because you have complete control over where and how your website is hosted.

With WordPress.org, you:

- **Choose Your Own Host:** Select a web hosting provider that fits your budget and performance needs.

- **Install Themes and Plugins Freely:** You can use any free or premium theme or plugin from thousands available.

- **Full Control Over Your Site:** Access all files and the database, allowing for unlimited customization and development.

- **Monetize Freely:** Sell products, run ads, or create membership sites without restrictions.

However, with this control comes responsibility. You are responsible for site maintenance, including security, backups, and upgrades. Luckily, many hosting providers now provide managed WordPress hosting that takes care of these technical details, making self-hosting much easier than in the past.

Which One Should You Choose?

For beginners wanting to develop a professional website or commercial presence, WordPress.org is often the suggested solution. The option to personalize and expand as your needs evolve is invaluable. It also gives enhanced SEO skills, e-commerce choices, and connection with other digital technologies.

WordPress.com is perfect if you want a rapid, hassle-free setup and don't anticipate needing sophisticated functionality or customization. If you are unsure, you can start with WordPress.com and eventually migrate to WordPress.org if your goals increase.

Why Choose WordPress in 2025? Latest Trends and Benefits

Choosing the right platform is vital for your website's success. Despite the rise of various website builders like Wix, Squarespace, and Shopify, WordPress remains the #1 choice for millions. Here's why WordPress stands strong in 2025 and what new developments make it more desirable than ever.

Unmatched Flexibility and Scalability

Whether you're building a personal blog, a portfolio site, a news source, or a huge online business, WordPress scales with your demands. The ability to add new functionality through plugins or even custom code means your site can expand over time without switching to a new platform.

In 2025, WordPress has sophisticated features like headless CMS settings, progressive web applications (PWAs), and easy connection with third-party APIs, making it future-proof for any company model.

Continued Improvement of the Block Editor

The Block Editor, introduced in 2018 and continuously developed, remains the center of content production in WordPress. It helps you to design complicated layouts graphically, utilizing blocks for text, photos, videos, buttons, and more. By 2025, the editor enables full site editing (FSE), meaning you may alter headers, footers, and other site elements with the same drag-and-drop ease used for pages.

This modern editing experience lowers reliance on various page builders and increases site speed and compatibility.

Strong Focus on Performance and Security

Speed and security are more crucial than ever in 2025. Google awards fast-loading sites with greater search ranks, and users demand flawless surfing on any device. WordPress core has made tremendous strides in optimizing performance, lowering page load times, and enhancing the overall user experience.

Security features have also been strengthened, with automated updates, improved password management, and greater integration with security plugins that guard against malware and hacking attempts.

Massive Community and Ecosystem

WordPress's global community is unmatched. Thousands of developers, designers, marketers, and educators contribute to its continuous growth. This means you have access to:

- **Thousands of Free and Premium Themes and Plugins:** Covering nearly every need imaginable.

- **Regular Updates:** Keeping your website compatible with new web standards and technologies.

- **Extensive Support Resources:** Tutorials, forums, webinars, and local meetups.

- **Integration with Popular Tools:** Email marketing services, CRM systems, payment gateways, and more.

SEO Friendly by Design

WordPress is built with search engines in mind. Clean, semantic code, easy URL customization, and a vast range of SEO plugins allow you to optimize your site effectively. In 2025, with the increasing importance of voice search and AI-driven content discovery, WordPress keeps pace by supporting schema markup, AMP pages, and fast mobile experiences.

Cost-Effective Solution

While WordPress.org needs money for hosting and domain registration, the platform itself is free. Compared to hiring developers or buying pricey proprietary software, WordPress offers good value for individuals and organizations of all sizes. Many important themes and plugins are free, while premium options are reasonable.

E-Commerce Powerhouse

With plugins like WooCommerce, WordPress turns into a comprehensive online store solution that competes with specialist systems. You may sell physical and digital products, manage inventory, set up subscriptions, and handle payments securely. In 2025, WooCommerce continues to innovate with new features supporting seamless shopping experiences and global payment choices.

Mobile-First and Accessibility Focused

WordPress themes and utilities increasingly focus on mobile responsiveness and accessibility. This ensures your site is usable and looks fantastic on smartphones, tablets, and accessible to those with disabilities—both critical aspects for reaching the biggest audience possible.

Understanding what WordPress is and why it remains the platform of choice for so many is the basis of your website-building journey. By choosing WordPress in 2025, you are investing in a flexible, powerful, and future-ready platform that grows with you.

Types of Websites You Can Build with WordPress

The range of websites you can construct with WordPress is enormous, making it a popular choice for various purposes. Whether your goal is simple or complex, WordPress can handle it.

1. Personal Blogs and Journals

At its inception, WordPress was designed as a blogging platform. It remains one of the best options for individuals who want to share their thoughts, stories, or expertise.

- **Features:** Easy post creation, comment sections, social sharing tools.

- **Uses:** Travel diaries, food blogs, parenting journals, creative writing.

- **Why WordPress:** Its intuitive editor allows bloggers to focus on writing without worrying about technical details.

2. Business Websites

Companies of all sizes use WordPress to establish their online presence.

- **Features:** Professional themes, service listings, contact forms, testimonials.

- **Uses:** Small businesses, startups, consultants, law firms.

- **Why WordPress:** Provides professional design and credibility while remaining budget-friendly.

3. Online Stores and E-Commerce

Thanks to plugins like WooCommerce, WordPress powers a significant number of online shops.

- **Features:** Product pages, shopping cart, secure payment gateways, inventory management.

- **Uses:** Selling physical goods, digital downloads, memberships, subscriptions.

- **Why WordPress:** Full control over store design and functionality with thousands of extensions.

4. Portfolios and Showcase Sites

Creative professionals — photographers, designers, artists — rely on WordPress to display their work.

- **Features:** Gallery layouts, image sliders, client testimonials, downloadable resumes.
- **Uses:** Portfolios, personal branding, freelance business showcases.
- **Why WordPress:** Customizable themes optimized for visual content highlight creative works beautifully.

5. Educational Websites and Online Courses

Educators and institutions use WordPress to offer courses and learning materials online.

- **Features:** Lesson plans, quizzes, student dashboards, membership controls.
- **Uses:** Online schools, tutoring services, course creators.
- **Why WordPress:** Plugins like LearnDash and LifterLMS turn WordPress into a powerful learning management system.

6. News and Magazine Websites

Media companies and bloggers build news portals with multiple categories and frequent updates.

- **Features:** Multi-author support, article categories, comment moderation, ad spaces.
- **Uses:** Online magazines, newspapers, niche news portals.
- **Why WordPress:** Supports high traffic and content-heavy sites with excellent organizational tools.

7. Community and Membership Sites

If you want to create a private or public community, WordPress can help.

- **Features:** User registration, forums, private content areas, subscription payments.
- **Uses:** Social groups, professional networks, clubs.

- **Why WordPress:** Plugins like BuddyPress and MemberPress make social networking and membership management straightforward.

8. Event and Booking Websites

Organize events and manage bookings effortlessly.

- **Features:** Event calendars, ticket sales, booking forms, reminders.
- **Uses:** Conferences, workshops, fitness classes, appointment bookings.
- **Why WordPress:** Enables easy event promotion and customer management with specialized plugins.

9. Nonprofit and Charity Websites

Many nonprofits use WordPress to raise awareness and collect donations.

- **Features:** Donation forms, volunteer signups, event promotion.
- **Uses:** Fundraising campaigns, community outreach.
- **Why WordPress:** Affordable, easy to manage, and supports fundraising tools.

10. Multilingual and International Websites

Reach audiences in multiple languages.

- **Features:** Language switchers, translated content, multilingual SEO.
- **Uses:** Global companies, tourism sites.
- **Why WordPress:** Plugins like WPML allow seamless multilingual content management.

These examples barely scratch the surface. Because WordPress is open-source and extensible, its capabilities grow continuously. From blogs to complex enterprise websites, WordPress adapts to fit your vision.

Overview of the WordPress Ecosystem

Building a website with WordPress is not just about installing software; it involves an ecosystem of components and a vibrant community. Understanding these parts will prepare you to harness WordPress's full potential.

Themes: Shaping Your Website's Appearance

Your website's theme controls how it looks and feels. Think of it as the skin or dress that wraps your content.

- **What Are Themes?** Themes define colors, fonts, layouts, header styles, menus, and overall design.

- **Free and Premium Themes:** Thousands of free themes are available in the WordPress theme directory, while premium themes offer advanced features and dedicated support.

- **Choosing a Theme:** Consider responsiveness (mobile-friendly), speed, SEO optimization, and compatibility with plugins.

- **Customization:** Modern themes offer customization options via the WordPress Customizer or dedicated theme panels.

- **Child Themes:** If you want to make deeper changes without losing the ability to update your theme, child themes allow safe modifications.

Plugins: Extending Your Site's Functionality

While WordPress provides basic website functionality out of the box, plugins add features and tools.

- **What Are Plugins?** Small software components you install to add capabilities like contact forms, SEO tools, social media integration, and more.

- **Installation and Management:** Easy to install via the WordPress dashboard with thousands available.

- **Must-Have Plugins:** Security plugins, caching tools for speed, SEO plugins like Yoast, and backup solutions.

- **Compatibility:** Choosing well-reviewed and regularly updated plugins is critical to avoid conflicts or security issues.

- **Custom Plugins:** Developers can build custom plugins to meet specific needs not covered by existing options.

Hosting: Where Your Website Lives

Every website needs a home — a server that stores its files and serves them to visitors online.

- **Types of Hosting:**
    - **Shared Hosting:** Affordable and beginner-friendly, but resources are shared with other websites.
    - **VPS Hosting:** Offers more resources and control for growing sites.
    - **Managed WordPress Hosting:** Specialized hosting optimized for WordPress, handling updates, backups, and performance.

- **Choosing a Host:** Consider uptime reliability, speed, customer support, and security features.

- **Domain Name:** Your website's address on the web, purchased separately or bundled with hosting.

- **SSL Certificates:** Essential for security and trust, SSL encrypts data and is often included with hosting plans.

The WordPress Community: Your Support Network

One of WordPress's greatest strengths is its global community.

- **Contributors:** Thousands of developers, designers, translators, and volunteers continuously improve WordPress core, themes, and plugins.

- **Support Forums:** The official WordPress support forums provide answers to countless questions.

- **Local Meetups and WordCamps:** Regular in-person and virtual gatherings offer learning and networking opportunities.

- **Documentation and Tutorials:** Extensive resources are available to help users at every skill level.

- **Open Source Philosophy:** The community-driven nature means WordPress evolves based on user needs and feedback.

The Continuous Evolution of WordPress

WordPress is not static; it grows and adapts with each update.

- **Regular Core Updates:** Keep your site secure and introduce new features.

- **Trends:** WordPress embraces modern web design standards, accessibility, and mobile-first development.

- **Integration:** Supports REST API and headless CMS setups for advanced developers.

- **Future Proof:** Designed to scale from small blogs to high-traffic enterprise sites.

Key Terminologies Every Beginner Must Know

Entering the world of WordPress without a grasp of its basic concepts can be like trying to read a foreign language without a dictionary. To help you feel more confident and equipped, here are some of the most significant terms you'll see frequently:

1. Content Management System (CMS)

A CMS is software that enables you to generate, edit, organize, and publish digital content without needing to code from scratch. WordPress is a CMS that allows users to manage everything from blog articles to full-fledged commercial websites through a user-friendly interface.

2. WordPress Core

This refers to the basic software package acquired from WordPress.org. The core includes the basic functions needed to run a website — such posting content, managing users, and setting site preferences. Everything else — themes, plugins, customizations — builds on this foundation.

3. Themes

Themes govern the visual style and layout of your website. They determine the look of your homepage, articles, navigation, colors, font, and more. Themes can be free or premium, and you can switch between them without losing your content.

4. Plugins

Plugins add unique features and increase the functionality of your WordPress site. Examples include contact forms, SEO tools, e-commerce capabilities, image galleries, and security measures. Plugins allow you to modify your site to match your unique needs.

5. Dashboard

The WordPress Dashboard is the administrative area where you manage your entire website. From the dashboard, you publish posts, install themes, manage users, and modify settings. It is your website's control center.

6. Posts vs. Pages

- **Posts** are entries listed in reverse chronological order and typically used for blog articles or news updates. They are dynamic and often organized by categories and tags.

- **Pages** are static content like "About Us," "Contact," or "Services" that don't change often and are usually organized in the site's navigation menus.

7. Categories and Tags

These are organizational tools to group and label posts:

- **Categories** are broad topics that help organize your content (e.g., "Recipes," "Travel").

- **Tags** are more specific keywords related to each post (e.g., "vegan," "Paris").

8. Permalinks

Permalinks are the permanent URLs for your pages and posts. A clean, descriptive permalink is important for both user experience and SEO. WordPress allows you to customize permalink structure for clarity and branding.

9. Widgets

Widgets are small blocks that add content and features to your site's sidebars, footers, or other widget-ready areas. Common widgets include recent posts, search bars, social media icons, and calendars.

10. Menus

Menus are navigational elements that guide visitors through your site. You create menus by adding pages, posts, custom links, or categories, and assign them to specific locations such as header or footer areas.

11. User Roles and Permissions

WordPress supports multiple user roles with varying levels of access:

- **Administrator:** Full control over the site.

- **Editor:** Can publish and manage posts/pages.

- **Author:** Can write and publish their own posts.

- **Contributor:** Can write posts but cannot publish.

- **Subscriber:** Can manage their profile but not create content.

Understanding these roles is vital when running a site with multiple contributors.

12. Shortcodes

Shortcodes are simple snippets of code that let you add complex features to posts or pages without coding knowledge. For example, inserting a gallery or embedding a video is often done using shortcodes.

13. Media Library

This is where you upload and manage images, videos, audio files, and documents that you use on your site.

14. SEO (Search Engine Optimization)

SEO involves optimizing your site to rank higher in search engine results. WordPress offers tools and plugins to help improve SEO through meta descriptions, keywords, sitemaps, and site speed.

15. Backups

Backups are copies of your website's files and database. Regular backups protect your site against data loss caused by mistakes, hacks, or server failures.

16. Caching

Caching stores temporary copies of your website's pages to speed up loading times for visitors. Proper caching improves user experience and search rankings.

17. SSL Certificate

SSL encrypts data transferred between your website and visitors, ensuring security. Sites with SSL display "https" in their URLs and are favored by search engines.

18. Hosting

Hosting is the service that stores your website's files on a server and makes your site accessible online.

19. Domain Name

Your website's address on the internet (e.g., www.yoursite.com).

20. Responsive Design

A design approach that ensures your website looks good and functions well on all devices, from desktops to smartphones.

Setting Realistic Expectations: What You Can Achieve as a Beginner

Starting a WordPress website is exciting, but it's important to enter the process with clear, realistic goals. Setting the right expectations helps prevent frustration and keeps you motivated.

What You Can Expect Early On

- **Learning Curve:** While WordPress is user-friendly, mastering its full capabilities takes time. Expect an initial learning curve as you become familiar with the dashboard, themes, and plugins.

- **Step-by-Step Progress:** Building a website is best approached as a series of manageable steps. You won't create a perfect site overnight; focus on gradual improvements.

- **Hands-On Practice:** The fastest way to learn is by doing. Experiment with settings, create posts, and customize themes as you learn.

- **Mistakes Are Part of the Journey:** You will encounter errors or issues — broken layouts, plugin conflicts, or slower page loads. These challenges are common and solvable.

What You Should Not Expect

- **No Coding Required, but Basic Tech Comfort Helps:** You don't need to be a developer, but basic familiarity with computers and the web is beneficial.

- **Instant Success:** Building traffic and engagement takes time. Content quality, SEO, and marketing efforts influence your site's reach.

- **One-Size-Fits-All Solutions:** Every site is unique. What works for others may need adjustment for your goals.

Achievable Goals in the First Weeks

- Set up your website with a domain and hosting.
- Install and configure WordPress.
- Choose and customize a theme.
- Create foundational pages: Home, About, Contact.
- Publish your first posts or products.

- Learn to manage media and plugins.
- Understand basic SEO settings.

Progressing Beyond the Basics

As you gain confidence, you can:

- Experiment with advanced themes and page builders.
- Add ecommerce functionality.
- Improve site speed and security.
- Build mailing lists and integrate marketing tools.
- Collaborate with contributors through user roles.

Staying Motivated and Avoiding Overwhelm

Many beginners feel overwhelmed by the number of choices in WordPress. To maintain motivation:

- **Break Tasks Into Small Pieces:** Focus on one step at a time.
- **Celebrate Small Wins:** Each published post or completed page is progress.
- **Use Community Resources:** Forums, tutorials, and local meetups can provide support.
- **Allow Time for Growth:** Websites evolve. Don't aim for perfection immediately.

Understanding basic WordPress terminologies and setting sensible expectations are your first tools on this website-building voyage. With time and practice, WordPress transforms from a scary platform into a strong ally, empowering you to communicate your message, sell things, or interact with your audience.

Chapter 2

Planning Your Website — Strategy Before Setup

Before you develop your website, it's vital to pause and plan. Building without a clear approach is like setting off on a journey without a destination - you could wander for hours, or worse, get lost completely. A well-thought-out plan not only saves you time and money but also ensures your website will accomplish your goals and connect with the proper audience.

Studies suggest that organizations with clearly defined online goals and strategies earn up to 30% higher engagement rates and conversions. Whether your goal is to share your passion, create a business, or establish an online brand, laying a solid foundation is crucial.

This chapter helps you establish your website's purpose, create measurable goals, and choose a domain and brand identity that will help you succeed.

Defining Your Website's Purpose and Goals

Every successful website starts with a simple question: Why am I establishing this site? The answer influences every decision — from design and content to marketing and monetization.

Common Website Purposes

Understanding common website types can help you articulate your own purpose.

- **Informational:** Sharing knowledge or news, like blogs, magazines, or educational sites.
- **E-commerce:** Selling products or services directly online.
- **Portfolio:** Showcasing your work, skills, or creative projects.
- **Community:** Building social networks, forums, or membership sites.
- **Lead Generation:** Collecting contact details to grow an audience or customer base.
- **Personal Branding:** Establishing yourself as an expert or influencer.
- **Event Promotion:** Advertising conferences, workshops, or local events.
- **Nonprofit/Charity:** Raising awareness and accepting donations.

How to Define Your Website's Purpose

Answer the following questions honestly and in detail:

- **What problem does my website solve?** Are you educating, entertaining, selling, or connecting people?

- **Who is my target audience?** Consider demographics, interests, and online behavior.

- **What action do I want visitors to take?** Buy a product, subscribe to a newsletter, contact you, or share content?

- **What sets my website apart?** Why should visitors choose your site over others?

Setting Clear, Measurable Goals

Goals provide direction and a way to measure success. They should be:

- **Specific:** Clearly defined rather than vague.

- **Measurable:** You can track progress with numbers or metrics.
- **Achievable:** Realistic given your resources.
- **Relevant:** Aligned with your overall vision.
- **Time-bound:** Set a timeline for achievement.

Examples of good website goals:

- Reach 5,000 monthly visitors within six months.
- Generate 100 email subscribers in the first quarter.
- Sell 50 products per month by year-end.
- Publish 2 new blog posts weekly.
- Secure 3 speaking engagements through the site within 12 months.

Aligning Content and Features with Goals

Once your goals are set, ensure every part of your website supports them:

- If your goal is to sell products, focus on e-commerce features and user-friendly checkout.
- For building community, prioritize membership tools and interactive forums.
- For branding, create an "About Me" page and showcase testimonials prominently.

Choosing the Right Domain Name and Brand Identity

Your domain name and brand identity are the cornerstones of your website's online presence. They impact how visitors perceive you, your credibility, and your ability to be found.

What Is a Domain Name?

Your domain is your website's address on the internet — the URL visitors type to reach you (e.g., www.yoursite.com). It should be easy to remember, spell, and relevant to your brand.

Tips for Choosing a Domain Name

- **Keep It Short and Simple:** Short names are easier to type and less prone to mistakes.

- **Make It Memorable:** Unique or catchy names stick in people's minds.

- **Use Keywords Wisely:** Including relevant keywords can help with search visibility, but don't sacrifice brand personality.

- **Avoid Numbers and Hyphens:** These often confuse users and can be mistyped.

- **Choose the Right Extension:** .com is the most recognized, but country-specific (.ng, .uk) or niche (.shop, .blog) extensions can work well depending on your focus.

- **Check Availability:** Use domain registrars to confirm your desired name isn't taken or trademarked.

Brainstorming Your Domain Name

- Start with a list of words related to your niche, values, or unique qualities.
- Combine words or create new ones (e.g., "Shopify," "WordPress").
- Use domain name generators online for ideas.
- Test your options by saying them out loud and asking friends for feedback.

Brand Identity: More Than Just a Logo

Brand identity encompasses everything that makes your website recognizable and relatable.

- **Logo:** A graphic symbol representing your brand.

- **Color Palette:** Colors that evoke your brand's personality (calm, energetic, trustworthy).

- **Typography:** Fonts that align with your message.

- **Voice and Tone:** How you communicate through text — formal, casual, humorous, or authoritative.

- **Imagery Style:** The kind of photos, icons, and graphics you use.

Why Brand Identity Matters

- Builds trust and professionalism.
- Creates emotional connections with your audience.
- Differentiates you from competitors.
- Enhances recall and loyalty.

How to Develop Your Brand Identity

- **Define Your Brand Personality:** If your website were a person, what traits would it have?

- **Research Competitors:** Identify what works and where you can stand out.

- **Create Mood Boards:** Collect colors, fonts, and images that reflect your style.

- **Design or Commission a Logo:** Use tools like Canva or hire designers on platforms like Fiverr or Upwork.

- **Apply Consistency:** Use your brand elements consistently across your website and marketing channels.

Protecting Your Brand

- Consider trademarking your brand name or logo.
- Purchase variations of your domain name to prevent confusion or misuse.
- Monitor your online presence regularly.

Practical Exercise: Define Your Website Strategy

Before moving on to setup, take time to write down your website's purpose, goals, desired visitor actions, and brand elements. This clarity will guide every subsequent decision.

- What is your website's primary purpose?
- Who is your target audience?
- What are your top three goals?
- List potential domain names.
- Describe your desired brand personality.

Taking the effort to plan your website's purpose and brand identity might seem like an extra step, but it pays off immensely in the long term. Clear goals keep your project focused and efficient, while a smart domain and brand generate a lasting impression on visitors.

Understanding Your Target Audience

Who are you constructing your website for? This inquiry isn't just about demographics; it's about understanding the motives, needs, and behaviors of your visitors.

Why Knowing Your Audience Matters

A website that resonates with its audience promotes engagement, builds trust, and achieves its goals. Without this knowledge, your site risks being irrelevant or confusing to visitors.

- **Enhances Content Relevance:** Knowing your audience guides the topics you cover and the language you use.

- **Improves User Experience:** Tailor navigation and features to visitor expectations.

- **Boosts Conversions:** Design calls-to-action (CTAs) that align with user intent.

- **Informs Marketing:** Target your promotional efforts effectively.

Steps to Define Your Target Audience

1. **Analyze Your Existing Customers or Community:** If you already have a business or social presence, start by reviewing your current followers or clients. What are their common traits?

2. **Create Audience Personas:** Build fictional profiles representing your typical users. Include age, occupation, interests, challenges, and goals.

3. **Identify Needs and Pain Points:** What problems does your audience face? How can your website help solve them?

4. **Consider User Behavior:** Where do they spend time online? What devices do they use? How tech-savvy are they?

5. **Research Competitors' Audiences:** Look at similar websites and note who engages with them and how.

Example Persona

Let's say you want to build a fitness blog aimed at busy professionals:

- **Name:** Sarah
- **Age:** 35
- **Occupation:** Marketing Manager
- **Needs:** Quick, effective workouts; healthy meal plans; stress management tips
- **Challenges:** Limited time, high stress, prefers mobile content
- **Goals:** Stay fit without sacrificing work or family time

Understanding Sarah guides you to create content like "10-minute workouts," "Meal prep hacks," and mobile-friendly videos.

Tools to Understand Your Audience

- **Google Analytics:** Provides demographics and behavior insights once your site is live.

- **Surveys and Polls:** Gather direct feedback via tools like SurveyMonkey or Google Forms.

- **Social Media Insights:** Platforms like Facebook and Instagram offer audience data.

- **Keyword Research:** Discover what your audience searches for using tools like Google Keyword Planner or Ubersuggest.

Planning Website Structure: Pages, Posts, Categories, and Menus

A well-organized website helps visitors find what they need quickly and keeps them engaged longer. WordPress offers several building blocks for organizing content — knowing how to use them is essential.

Pages vs. Posts: What's the Difference?

- **Pages** are static content, typically used for evergreen information that doesn't change often.
    - Examples: About Us, Contact, Services, Privacy Policy.
- **Posts** are dynamic entries displayed in reverse chronological order, perfect for regularly updated content.
    - Examples: Blog articles, news updates, announcements.

Using pages and posts appropriately helps keep your website clear and user-friendly.

Categories and Tags: Organizing Your Posts

WordPress lets you classify posts using **categories** and **tags** to help visitors and search engines understand your content.

- **Categories** group broad topics or themes.
    - Example: A travel blog might have categories like "Europe," "Asia," "Adventure," "Food."
- **Tags** are specific keywords related to a post's content.
    - Example: Under "Europe," a post could be tagged with "Paris," "Museums," "Budget travel."

Effective use of categories and tags improves navigation and SEO.

Creating Your Website's Page Structure

Before building, sketch out your main pages and how they relate to each other. A simple hierarchy might look like this:

- Home
- About
- Blog
    - Category 1

        - Category 2
    - Services/Product
    - Contact

Crafting Menus for Easy Navigation

Menus guide visitors to key parts of your site. Plan your main menu with essential pages and categories. Use submenus for organization without clutter.

Keep menus intuitive — avoid too many items, and prioritize important content.

Planning for Scalability

As your site grows, new content will require new categories, pages, and menu items. Build your structure flexibly to allow easy expansion.

Creating a Content Strategy: What to Publish and When

Publishing content isn't just about quantity; it's about delivering value consistently to your audience.

Why a Content Strategy Matters

- **Attracts and Retains Visitors:** Regular, relevant content keeps your site fresh and engaging.

- **Supports SEO:** Targeted content improves your site's search engine ranking.

- **Builds Authority:** High-quality content establishes your expertise and trustworthiness.

- **Drives Conversions:** Guides visitors toward desired actions.

Defining Your Content Goals

Link your content to your website goals. For example:

- If building brand awareness, focus on informative blog posts and social media sharing.
- For e-commerce, publish product guides, reviews, and customer stories.
- To build community, create interactive content like polls, forums, and live streams.

Planning Content Types

Consider varying formats to keep your audience engaged:

- Blog articles
- Videos
- Infographics
- Podcasts
- Case studies
- Tutorials and guides
- News and updates

Building an Editorial Calendar

Schedule your content production and publication to maintain consistency. Plan topics ahead, assign deadlines, and track progress.

Frequency and Timing

Choose a publishing frequency you can sustain — quality over quantity is crucial. Posting once or twice a week often works well for beginners.

Use analytics and audience insights to determine the best times to publish for your audience.

Content Ideation Tips

- Answer common questions your audience asks.
- Solve problems and provide actionable tips.
- Share stories or case studies to humanize your brand.
- Use keyword research to identify trending topics.

Practical Exercise: Mapping Your Website Strategy

To help you prepare, create a document answering:

- Who is my target audience? Describe their traits and needs.
- What is my website's primary structure? List planned pages and categories.
- What types of content will I produce? How often?
- What are my short-term and long-term content goals?

Taking time to study your audience, organize your site's structure, and develop a content strategy sets you apart from those that construct websites on impulse. A thoughtful plan results in a more effective, engaging, and successful website.

Wireframing Your Site Layout: Tools and Techniques for Beginners

Wireframing is the process of developing a skeletal layout of your website's pages and user interface. Think of it as the architectural layout for a structure – it doesn't display the final colors or textures, but it outlines where walls, doors, and windows go.

Why Wireframe?

- **Visual Clarity:** Wireframes help you and your team (or yourself) visualize the layout and content arrangement.

- **Identify User Flow:** You can plan how visitors will move through your site and access information.

- **Spot Gaps Early:** Avoid costly redesigns by catching layout or usability issues before building.

- **Focus on Functionality:** Wireframes prioritize user experience and functionality over design flair.

- **Efficient Communication:** They serve as a reference when working with designers, developers, or content creators.

Key Elements of a Wireframe

- **Header:** Usually includes logo placement, navigation menu, and contact info or call-to-action buttons.

- **Hero Section:** The prominent area visitors see first — often a banner image, headline, or introductory message.

- **Content Blocks:** Sections for text, images, videos, or interactive elements.

- **Sidebar (Optional):** Secondary navigation or additional content like recent posts or ads.

- **Footer:** Contains contact info, links, social media icons, and legal disclaimers.

- **Buttons and Links:** Calls-to-action prompting users to take specific steps.

Wireframes typically use simple shapes and placeholder text to represent these elements.

Wireframing Techniques for Beginners

1. Paper and Pen

The simplest and most accessible method — sketch your layout ideas on paper.

- Draw boxes representing headers, images, text blocks, and buttons.
- Experiment with different arrangements.
- Annotate with notes about functionality or content.

Pros: Fast, tactile, no software needed.

Cons: Harder to share digitally or make precise changes.

2. Whiteboard Sessions

If you work with a team or want to brainstorm ideas, a whiteboard is perfect.

- Quickly sketch layouts and flow diagrams.
- Encourage collaboration and instant feedback.
- Capture photos of your work for future reference.

---

3. Digital Wireframing Tools

As you grow comfortable, move to digital tools that allow for cleaner, editable wireframes.

Some beginner-friendly options include:

- **Figma:** Free and cloud-based, great for collaborative work.

- **Balsamiq:** Offers a hand-drawn style to focus on structure, not design.

- **Adobe XD:** Powerful and widely used for UX design.

- **Wireframe.cc:** Minimalist and simple interface for quick wireframes.

- **Canva:** Though primarily for graphics, it can be used to mock up layouts with drag-and-drop elements.

Creating Your First Wireframe: Step-by-Step

1. **Define Your Goal:** Start with the purpose of the page (e.g., home page to introduce brand and capture leads).

2. **List Key Elements:** Identify must-have features like logo, menu, main headline, content sections, contact info.

3. **Sketch the Layout:** Arrange elements logically — think about visual hierarchy and flow.

4. **Consider User Actions:** Where will visitors click? What paths should they follow?

5. **Review and Refine:** Get feedback from others or revisit your wireframe to improve clarity.

Wireframing Tips for WordPress Beginners

- Focus on **user experience (UX)**, ensuring visitors can find information easily.
- Keep **consistency** in layouts to avoid confusing visitors.
- Start with low-fidelity wireframes (simple sketches) before moving to detailed ones.
- Consider **mobile layouts** early — many visitors will access your site on phones.
- Use wireframes as a **reference** when selecting themes and plugins.

Checklist: Preparing for a Successful WordPress Launch

With your wireframe ready, preparing for launch is your next essential process. Launching without a checklist is perilous – even little oversights can lead to broken connections, missing pictures, or security risks.

Here is a detailed pre-launch checklist designed to guide beginners through a smooth, confident WordPress launch.

1. Technical Setup

- **Domain and Hosting:** Confirm your domain registration and hosting plan are active.
- **WordPress Installation:** Install WordPress either manually or via one-click installers from your host.
- **SSL Certificate:** Set up SSL to secure your site with HTTPS.
- **Permalink Settings:** Configure user-friendly URL structures in WordPress settings.

2. Theme and Design

- **Theme Installation:** Install and activate your chosen theme.
- **Customize Appearance:** Set colors, fonts, logos, and layouts matching your wireframe.
- **Mobile Responsiveness:** Test your design on various devices and screen sizes.
- **Browser Compatibility:** Check your site on multiple browsers (Chrome, Firefox, Safari).

3. Content Preparation

- **Pages Created:** Build essential pages such as Home, About, Contact, Privacy Policy.
- **Content Edited:** Proofread all text, check for grammar and clarity.
- **Images Optimized:** Use compressed images for faster loading without quality loss.
- **Placeholders Removed:** Ensure no lorem ipsum or filler text remains.
- **SEO Metadata Added:** Titles and meta descriptions added using SEO plugins.

4. Functionality Checks

- **Navigation Menus:** Test all links and menus for proper redirection.

- **Forms Tested:** Ensure contact forms and subscription forms work correctly.

- **Plugin Configuration:** Activate and configure essential plugins for SEO, caching, and security.

- **Broken Links Scanned:** Use tools to detect and fix any broken links.

- **Load Time Tested:** Check website speed with tools like GTmetrix or Google PageSpeed Insights.

5. Security Measures

- **Strong Passwords:** Use complex passwords for all admin accounts.

- **Limit Login Attempts:** Use plugins to prevent brute-force attacks.

- **Backup Setup:** Install backup plugins and schedule regular backups.

- **Firewall and Malware Scans:** Activate security plugins and perform scans.

6. Legal and Compliance

- **Privacy Policy Page:** Create a clear privacy policy explaining data handling.

- **Cookie Consent:** Add cookie notifications if your audience is in jurisdictions requiring consent.

- **Terms and Conditions:** Include site rules and disclaimers if applicable.

- **GDPR Compliance:** Ensure compliance with data protection laws if relevant.

7. Analytics and Tracking

- **Google Analytics Installed:** Set up analytics to monitor visitor behavior.

- **Search Console Connected:** Connect your site with Google Search Console.

- **Conversion Tracking:** Set up goals and events for measuring actions like form submissions or sales.

8. Final Pre-Launch Testing

- **Cross-Device Testing:** Check website appearance and functionality on mobile, tablet, and desktop.

- **User Testing:** Ask friends or colleagues to browse your site and provide feedback.

- **Accessibility Check:** Ensure your site meets basic accessibility standards.

- **Review Backup and Recovery:** Test backup restoration processes.

9. Launch and Post-Launch Plans

- **Set Launch Date:** Plan a soft launch to fix any unforeseen issues.

- **Announce Launch:** Prepare marketing messages for email lists and social media.

- **Monitor Site Performance:** Use analytics to observe traffic and behavior.

- **Prepare for Updates:** Schedule regular updates for WordPress core, themes, and plugins.

Practical Exercise: Create Your Wireframe and Launch Checklist

Use the following worksheet to organize your thoughts:

- **Draw your Home page layout:** Sketch header, hero section, content blocks, footer.

- **List essential pages and their purposes.**

- **Write down navigation menu items.**

- **Create a checklist covering all launch steps above with deadlines.**

Wireframing and prepping with a comprehensive checklist are the cornerstones of a successful WordPress website launch. They ensure your vision converts into a practical, user-friendly site that achieves your goals.

By embracing these planning strategies, you position yourself to avoid typical pitfalls and design a site that serves your audience successfully from day one.

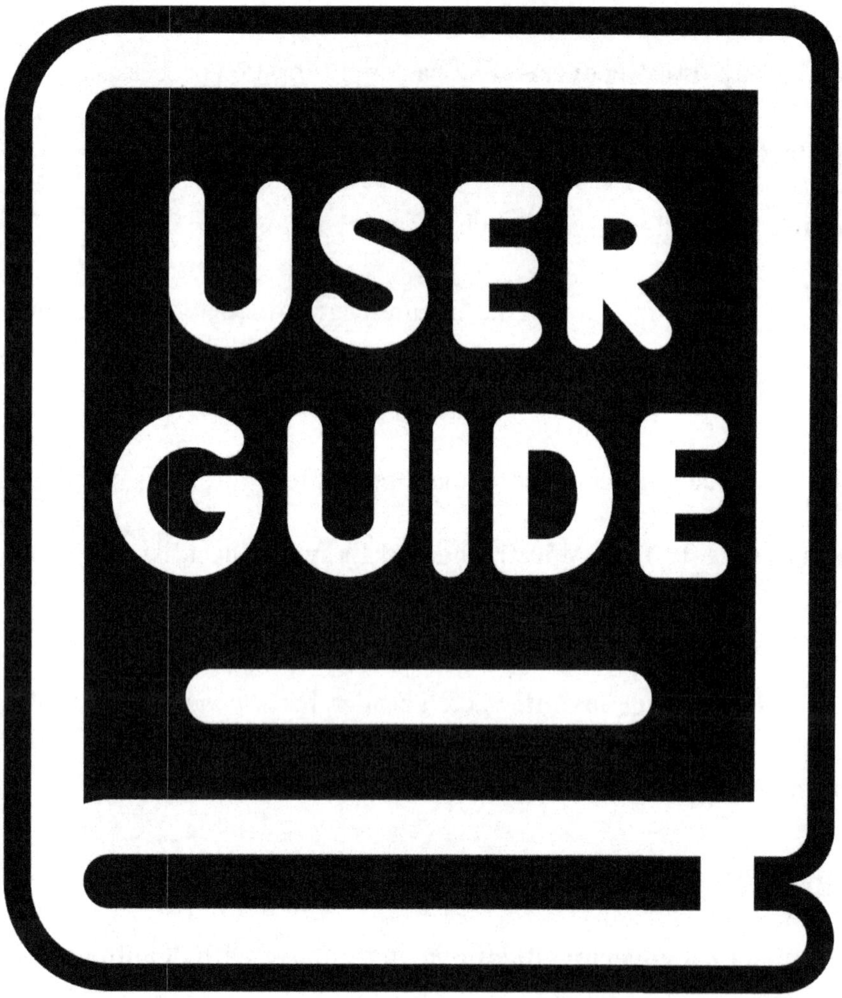
USER
GUIDE

Chapter 3

Setting Up Your WordPress Site from Scratch

Did you know that over 90% of successful websites owe part of their performance and security to a reputable hosting provider? Before your WordPress website can greet visitors, it needs a home on the internet. Choosing the correct hosting and getting a domain name are the critical initial stages in bringing your site to life.

In this chapter, you will discover how to select the hosting that meets your individual needs and the detailed procedure of registering your domain and setting up DNS – the technical yet manageable basis for your WordPress journey.

Choosing the Best Hosting Provider for Your Needs

Hosting is where your website files, graphics, databases, and content live, making your site available 24/7 to visitors across the globe. The quality of your hosting affects your site's speed, security, uptime, and even SEO.

There is no one-size-fits-all hosting option. Your option relies on your budget, website size, estimated traffic, and technical comfort level. Below is an in-depth look at the three main hosting kinds offered to WordPress users: Shared, VPS, and Managed WordPress Hosting.

Shared Hosting: The Beginner's Entry Point

Shared hosting is the most affordable and user-friendly option, making it popular among beginners, bloggers, and small businesses just starting out.

- **How it works:** Your website shares a physical server and its resources (CPU, RAM, bandwidth) with many other websites.

- **Pros:** Low cost, simple setup, basic support, easy control panel.

- **Cons:** Limited resources, potential slower speeds during traffic spikes, less control over server settings.

- **Best for:** Small personal blogs, portfolios, and low-traffic sites.

Many hosting companies offer one-click WordPress installation with shared hosting plans, making setup seamless.

VPS Hosting (Virtual Private Server): More Power and Control

VPS hosting divides a physical server into multiple virtual servers, each isolated from others. It offers dedicated resources and greater control.

- **How it works:** You get a slice of server resources exclusively yours, improving performance and stability.

- **Pros:** Better speed, scalability, root access, customizable server environment.

- **Cons:** More expensive than shared hosting, requires some technical knowledge.

- **Best for:** Growing websites, businesses needing higher performance and security.

VPS hosting is ideal if you expect steady traffic growth or need custom configurations.

Managed WordPress Hosting: Stress-Free Optimization

Managed WordPress hosting is a specialized service where the provider handles all technical aspects, including WordPress updates, backups, caching, and security.

- **How it works:** Optimized servers specifically designed for WordPress, with automated maintenance.

- **Pros:** Automatic updates and backups, enhanced security, expert WordPress support, superior performance.

- **Cons:** Higher cost compared to shared hosting, some limitations on plugins or customizations.

- **Best for:** Businesses, e-commerce sites, those who prefer to focus on content and marketing rather than technical details.

Many managed hosts provide staging environments, CDN integration, and performance analytics, valuable for professional sites.

Key Factors to Consider When Choosing Hosting

1. **Reliability and Uptime:** Aim for providers guaranteeing 99.9% uptime to ensure your site stays accessible.

2. **Speed and Performance:** Fast loading sites retain visitors and rank higher on Google.

3. **Customer Support:** 24/7 expert support is crucial, especially for beginners.

4. **Security Features:** Look for SSL certificates, firewalls, malware scanning, and DDoS protection.

5. **Scalability:** Choose a provider that can grow with your website's needs.

6. **Control Panel:** A user-friendly control panel (like cPanel or custom dashboards) simplifies management.

7. **Backup Services:** Regular automated backups protect your data.

8. **Pricing and Renewal Rates:** Understand introductory prices and renewal fees.

Popular Hosting Providers to Consider in 2025

- **Bluehost:** Recommended by WordPress.org, beginner-friendly with shared and managed plans.

- **SiteGround:** Known for excellent support and performance.

- **WP Engine:** Premium managed WordPress hosting for businesses.

- **HostGator:** Affordable shared hosting with easy WordPress setup.

- **Kinsta:** High-performance managed hosting with Google Cloud infrastructure.

Step-by-Step Domain Registration and DNS Setup

Your domain name is your website's address on the internet – the memorable name customers type into their browsers to locate you. Registering and configuring your domain properly is key.

What is Domain Registration?

Domain registration reserves your unique website name for a specified duration, often one year, with the opportunity to renew. Registrars are firms accredited to offer domain names.

Step 1: Choose Your Domain Name

Refer to Chapter 2 for domain naming best practices: short, memorable, and relevant names are excellent. Use domain name registrars to check availability.

Step 2: Select a Domain Registrar

Some popular domain registrars include:

- GoDaddy
- Namecheap
- Google Domains
- Bluehost (often bundled with hosting)

Step 3: Register Your Domain

- Create an account on your chosen registrar's site.
- Search for your desired domain name.
- Add it to your cart and proceed to checkout.
- Provide registrant details (name, email, address).
- Opt for privacy protection to shield personal info.
- Complete payment.

Step 4: Understand DNS (Domain Name System)

DNS translates your domain name into the IP address of your hosting server, directing visitors to your website.

Step 5: Configure DNS Settings

If your domain registrar and hosting are the same company, DNS settings are usually auto-configured.

If they differ:

- **Obtain Nameservers from Hosting Provider:** Nameservers are addresses like ns1.examplehost.com.

- **Update Nameservers in Domain Registrar Account:** Replace default nameservers with those provided.

- **Propagation Time:** DNS changes take from a few minutes to 48 hours to propagate globally.

Step 6: Verify Domain Connection

After DNS propagation:

- Visit your domain URL to check if your hosting server responds.
- Use online tools like "WhatsMyDNS.net" to check propagation status.
- If issues persist, verify name server accuracy or contact support.

Step 7: Set Up SSL Certificate

SSL certificates encrypt data for security and display a padlock in browsers.

- Many hosts offer free SSL (via Let's Encrypt).
- Activate SSL in the hosting control panel.
- Configure WordPress to use HTTPS URLs (plugins like Really Simple SSL help).

Troubleshooting Common Domain Issues

- **Domain Not Resolving:** Check nameserver settings and wait for propagation.
- **Wrong Website Displays:** Clear browser cache or confirm correct hosting setup.
- **SSL Errors:** Ensure SSL is installed and WordPress URL settings use HTTPS.

Practical Exercise: Register Your Domain and Connect to Hosting

Follow these steps hands-on:

- Choose and register your domain via a registrar.
- Select a hosting plan suited to your needs.
- Update domain nameservers if registrar and host differ.
- Confirm domain points to your hosting.
- Enable SSL for security.

Selecting the ideal hosting and properly registering your domain lay the groundwork for a successful WordPress website. Thoughtful hosting selections ensure your site functions properly, while meticulous domain configuration helps visitors discover you without problem.

One-Click WordPress Installation vs Manual Installation

Installing WordPress is the doorway to your site. How you get WordPress operating relies on your hosting provider and your comfort with technical activities.

One-Click WordPress Installation

One-click installation is a simplified, automated process offered by most modern hosting companies. It drastically decreases setup time and complexity, making it suitable for novices.

- **How it works:** Your hosting control panel (such as cPanel or custom dashboards) provides an application installer like Softaculous, Fantastico, or Installatron. With a few clicks, WordPress files are downloaded, the database created, and your admin account set up automatically.

- **Steps for One-Click Installation:**

    - Log into your hosting control panel.
    - Locate the WordPress installer under the "Website" or "Apps" section.
    - Click "Install" and select your domain.
    - Fill in site title, admin username, password, and email.
    - Choose language and desired settings.
    - Click "Install" and wait a few minutes.
    - Receive confirmation and login credentials.

- **Advantages:**
  - Fast and easy, requires no coding.
  - Reduces risk of errors.
  - Usually configures basic settings automatically.

- **Limitations:**
  - Limited customization during setup.
  - May not be available on all hosting platforms.

Manual WordPress Installation

Manual installation involves downloading WordPress files, uploading them to your server, and configuring databases yourself. It requires more technical skill but offers full control.

- **When to use manual installation:**
  - Your host doesn't support one-click installers.
  - You need custom configurations or multi-site setups.
  - You prefer hands-on control.

- **Step-by-step manual installation:**
  - **Download WordPress:**
    - Visit WordPress.org and download the latest package.
  - **Upload Files to Server:**
    - Use FTP clients like FileZilla or your hosting file manager to upload WordPress files to your domain's root directory (usually public_html).
  - **Create a Database:**
    - In your hosting control panel, access MySQL Database Wizard.
    - Create a new database and user with full privileges.
    - Save credentials securely.

- **Configure wp-config.php:**
  - Rename wp-config-sample.php to wp-config.php.
  - Edit with your database name, username, password, and host.

- **Run the Installation Script:**
  - Visit your domain (e.g., www.yoursite.com).
  - Follow on-screen instructions to set site title, admin user, password, and email.

- **Advantages:**
  - Full control over installation.
  - Allows advanced customizations.

- **Challenges:**
  - More complex, higher risk of errors.
  - Requires familiarity with FTP and database management.

Exploring the WordPress Dashboard: First Look and Overview

Once installed, WordPress opens the door to your website's heart—the Dashboard. This central hub lets you manage content, design, settings, and users.

Getting to the Dashboard

Access the Dashboard by visiting www.yoursite.com/wp-admin and logging in with your admin credentials.

Dashboard Components

- **Admin Toolbar:** The top black bar offering quick links to your site, new post creation, and profile settings.

- **Sidebar Menu:** The main navigation on the left with expandable menus including Posts, Media, Pages, Comments, Appearance, Plugins, Users, Tools, and Settings.

- **Welcome Widget:** Offers shortcuts to common tasks like writing your first post or customizing your site.

- **At a Glance:** Displays site statistics such as number of posts, pages, comments, and current WordPress version.

- **Activity:** Shows recent posts, comments, and upcoming scheduled content.

- **Quick Draft:** Allows you to jot down ideas or start posts rapidly.

- **News:** Updates from the WordPress community and development team.

Key Areas in Detail

1. Posts

Manage blog articles or news items here. Add, edit, categorize, and tag posts to organize your content.

2. Media

The media library stores your images, videos, PDFs, and other uploads. Easily insert media into posts and pages.

3. Pages

Create static pages like "About" or "Contact." Unlike posts, pages are hierarchical and usually appear in navigation menus.

4. Comments

View, approve, or delete comments from visitors. Moderate discussions to maintain a positive community.

5. Appearance

Control site design elements:

- **Themes:** Install or switch themes.
- **Customize:** Access the WordPress Customizer for colors, logos, menus.
- **Widgets:** Add content blocks to sidebars and footers.

- **Menus:** Create and assign navigation menus.

6. Plugins

Manage plugins to add or remove features. Search the plugin repository, install new plugins, and configure settings.

7. Users

Add or edit user profiles and assign roles like Administrator, Editor, or Subscriber.

8. Settings

The control center for your site's basic configuration, including general settings, writing options, reading preferences, discussion, media, and permalinks.

Essential Settings: General, Permalinks, Reading, and Discussion

After exploring your Dashboard, configuring essential settings tailors your site's behavior and optimizes visitor experience.

General Settings

Found under **Settings > General**, this section includes:

- **Site Title:** The name of your website, displayed in browser tabs and headers.
- **Tagline:** A brief description or slogan.
- **WordPress Address (URL) & Site Address (URL):** Usually your domain name; change only if migrating sites.
- **Email Address:** For admin notifications.
- **Membership:** Choose whether visitors can register accounts.
- **New User Default Role:** Set default role for new users.
- **Timezone, Date Format, Time Format:** Adjust to your location and preferences.
- **Site Language:** Select the language WordPress displays in.

Make sure these are accurate to establish your site's identity.

Permalinks Settings

Under **Settings** > **Permalinks**, configure how URLs appear. Clean, descriptive URLs improve usability and SEO.

Common choices:

- **Plain:** Numeric URLs (not recommended).
- **Day and Name / Month and Name:** Includes date in URLs, good for news sites.
- **Post Name:** Uses the post or page title, favored for blogs and business sites.
- **Custom Structure:** For advanced URL customization.

Choosing "Post Name" is a widely recommended option for beginners seeking simplicity and SEO benefits.

Reading Settings

Located under **Settings** > **Reading**, these control your homepage and post display:

- **Homepage Displays:** Choose between displaying your latest posts or a static page.

- **Blog Pages Show at Most:** Number of posts per page.

- **Syndication Feeds Show the Most Recent:** Limits posts shown in RSS feeds.

- **For Each Article in a Feed, Show:** Full text or summary.

- **Search Engine Visibility:** Option to discourage search engines from indexing your site (useful for development stages).

Configure this to match your website's goals, whether a blog or business homepage.

Discussion Settings

Found under **Settings** > **Discussion**, these manage comments and interaction:

- **Default Article Settings:** Control notifications for linkbacks and pingbacks.

- **Other Comment Settings:** Options for comment author requirements, threading, moderation.

- **Email Me Whenever:** Notify admins of comments or moderation needs.

- **Before a Comment Appears:** Options for manual approval or automatic approval.

- **Comment Moderation and Blacklist:** Rules to filter spam or inappropriate comments.

- **Avatars:** Display user avatars and control their ratings.

Moderating comments maintains quality discussion and protects against spam.

Practical Exercise: Configure Your Essential Settings

Take time to:

- Set your site title and tagline.
- Choose your preferred permalink structure.
- Decide if you want a static homepage or blog feed.
- Adjust comment settings according to your audience.

Setting up WordPress from scratch could seem difficult, but with guided steps, it becomes simple and even thrilling. Choosing between one-click and manual installations depends on your technical comfort, while the Dashboard becomes your command center. Essential settings dictate how your site runs and presents itself, making this core knowledge vital.

Understanding WordPress User Roles and Permissions

WordPress's multi-user capabilities allow numerous individuals to contribute on your website, each with preset access levels. This approach helps maintain your site structured, secure, and efficient.

Why User Roles Matter

Imagine a bustling office: everyone has a different job, and not all employees require the keys to every door. User roles in WordPress work similarly. They ensure that only the right personnel have access to critical regions, preventing accidental or malicious alterations.

For a single-person website, this may seem unneeded, but as your site expands, introducing contributors, editors, or developers becomes frequent – making user roles important.

The Default WordPress User Roles

WordPress comes with five default user roles, each with a specific set of permissions.

1. Administrator

- **Capabilities:** Full access to all administrative features and settings.
- **Ideal for:** Site owners or trusted individuals managing the entire website.
- **Responsibilities:** Managing themes, plugins, users, settings, content, and updates.

Because of their power, administrator accounts must be tightly secured.

2. Editor

- **Capabilities:** Can publish and manage posts, including those written by others.
- **Ideal for:** Content managers or editors in charge of reviewing and approving posts.
- **Limitations:** Cannot change site settings or install themes/plugins.

3. Author

- **Capabilities:** Can write, edit, publish, and delete their own posts.
- **Ideal for:** Freelance writers or contributors who produce content independently.
- **Limitations:** Cannot edit others' content or site settings.

4. Contributor

- **Capabilities:** Can write and edit their own posts but cannot publish.
- **Ideal for:** Guest writers or interns needing editorial review before publication.
- **Limitations:** Cannot upload media or access site settings.

5. Subscriber

- **Capabilities:** Can only manage their user profile.
- **Ideal for:** Registered site visitors, newsletter subscribers, or members.
- **Limitations:** No content editing or publishing rights.

Customizing Roles and Permissions

While default roles cover most needs, WordPress allows for role customization through plugins like **User Role Editor** or **Members**. You can tailor capabilities, create new roles, or restrict access further.

For example, you might create a **SEO Manager** role with permissions to manage SEO plugins but no access to content editing.

Best Practices for Managing User Roles

- **Limit Administrators:** Only assign administrator rights to people you trust completely.
- **Use Appropriate Roles:** Assign the lowest level of access necessary for a user's tasks.
- **Regularly Review Users:** Audit accounts to remove inactive or unnecessary users.
- **Educate Users:** Ensure users understand their permissions and security responsibilities.

Security Best Practices from Day One: Passwords, SSL, and Backups

Security should never be an afterthought. Implementing foundational security measures from the start protects your site, your data, and your visitors.

Strong Passwords: The First Line of Defense

Weak or reused passwords are the most common cause of website breaches. A single compromised password can expose your entire site.

Creating Strong Passwords

- Use a mix of uppercase, lowercase, numbers, and special characters.
- Aim for passwords longer than 12 characters.
- Avoid dictionary words, common phrases, or easily guessable information.
- Use unique passwords for each account.

Password Management Tools

Managing complex passwords can be daunting. Password managers like **LastPass**, **1Password**, or **Bitwarden** securely store and autofill passwords.

Enforcing Strong Passwords in WordPress

Plugins like **Force Strong Passwords** require users to create secure passwords during registration or profile updates.

Two-Factor Authentication (2FA)

Adding a second verification step greatly increases login security.

- Common methods include authentication apps (Google Authenticator, Authy) or email/SMS codes.

- Many plugins like **Google Authenticator** or **Wordfence** support 2FA integration.

SSL Certificates: Securing Data Transmission

SSL (Secure Sockets Layer) encrypts the connection between your website and visitors, protecting sensitive data such as login credentials, payment information, and personal details.

Why SSL Matters

- **Security:** Encrypts data, preventing interception.
- **SEO:** Google favors HTTPS-enabled sites.
- **Trust:** Modern browsers display padlocks for secure sites, reassuring visitors.

Obtaining and Installing SSL

- Many hosting providers offer free SSL via **Let's Encrypt**.
- Installation is often automatic on managed hosts.
- Use plugins like **Really Simple SSL** to enable HTTPS across your WordPress site.

Regular Backups: Your Safety Net

Despite precautions, accidents and attacks happen. Having a backup ensures you can restore your site to a working state quickly.

Backup Essentials

- Backup both **files** (themes, plugins, uploads) and the **database** (content, settings).

- Automate backups with plugins like **UpdraftPlus**, **BackupBuddy**, or hosting provider tools.

- Store backups off-site (cloud storage or separate servers) to avoid data loss.

Backup Frequency

- For static sites, weekly backups might suffice.

- For dynamic sites with frequent changes (blogs, stores), daily or even real-time backups are advisable.

Additional Security Measures

- **Limit Login Attempts:** Prevent brute force attacks by restricting failed login attempts.

- **Disable File Editing:** Prevent unauthorized users from editing theme or plugin files via the dashboard.

- **Keep WordPress Updated:** Regularly update WordPress core, themes, and plugins.

- **Use Security Plugins:** Tools like **Wordfence** or **Sucuri** provide firewalls, malware scans, and monitoring.

- **Secure Hosting:** Choose hosts with strong security policies and proactive monitoring.

Practical Exercise: Secure Your WordPress Site

- Create a unique, strong administrator password.
- Enable two-factor authentication.
- Install SSL and force HTTPS.
- Set up automated daily backups.
- Install and configure a security plugin.

Managing user roles carefully and establishing solid security policies from the start guard your WordPress website against numerous common threats and operational issues. These precautions protect your content, your visitors, and your reputation.

With these foundations built, you can build confidently, knowing your site is safe, organized, and ready to grow.

Chapter 4

Mastering the WordPress Block Editor (Gutenberg)

Since its release in 2018, the WordPress Block Editor, often known as Gutenberg, has changed how websites are designed and content is created. By 2025, it has become the standard for editing WordPress content, empowering beginners and professionals alike to construct rich, dynamic pages without touching a line of code.

Did you know that over 90% of WordPress sites now use the Block Editor? This movement signifies a move away from the standard text editor towards a modular, adaptable system that puts creativity and power into your hands.

This chapter goes deep into the Block Editor's interface and leads you through the basic blocks that constitute the building blocks of your content.

Introduction to the Block Editor Interface

At first sight, the WordPress Block Editor could feel like walking into a new planet. Unlike the traditional single-text box editor, the Block Editor separates your page or post into individual components called "blocks," each responsible for a certain piece of content or function.

Understanding the Block Concept

Think of blocks as Lego pieces. Each block represents a piece of your content – a text, image, list, or quote — and you stack and organize these blocks to form your page.

This modular system gives you:

- **Flexibility:** Rearrange blocks easily to change layout.
- **Consistency:** Each block behaves predictably with uniform settings.
- **Extensibility:** Developers can create custom blocks for specialized needs.

The Main Components of the Block Editor Interface

When you open the editor, here's what you'll see:

1. Top Toolbar

This horizontal bar at the top provides:

- **Save Draft/Publish:** Save or publish your work.
- **Preview:** View how your content looks on the front end.
- **Settings Toggle:** Show or hide the sidebar.
- **Undo/Redo:** Step backward or forward through edits.
- **Content Structure:** Displays word count and heading outline.
- **Block Navigation:** Quickly jump between blocks.

2. Sidebar

On the right side, the sidebar holds two tabs:

- **Document:** Settings for the entire post/page — status, visibility, categories, tags, featured image, permalink.

- **Block:** Settings specific to the currently selected block — alignment, color, typography, spacing.

3. Content Area

This central space is where you add and edit blocks. Click the + icon to add a new block anywhere.

4. Block Toolbar

When you select a block, a contextual toolbar appears above it with controls like alignment, formatting, and more.

How to Access the Block Editor

To create or edit content using the Block Editor:

- Go to your WordPress Dashboard.
- Click **Posts > Add New** or **Pages > Add New**.
- The Block Editor opens by default in modern WordPress installations.

59

- You can also edit existing content by clicking the edit button.

Using Basic Blocks: Paragraph, Heading, Image, Lists, Quotes

Blocks come in many types, but mastering the basics gives you the confidence to build any content layout.

Paragraph Block: The Building Block of Text

The **Paragraph block** is where you write your main text content.

- **Adding a Paragraph Block:** Click the + button and select **Paragraph**, or simply start typing.

- **Formatting Options:** Use the block toolbar to apply bold, italic, links, inline code, or strikethrough.

- **Alignment:** Align text left, center, or right.

- **Text Color:** Customize color and background color.

- **Typography:** Adjust font size and drop cap.

- **Spacing:** Modify padding and margins (depending on theme support).

Tips:

- Press **Enter** to add a new paragraph block.

- Use keyboard shortcuts like **Ctrl + B** for bold and **Ctrl + I** for italic.

- Keep paragraphs short for readability.

Heading Block: Structuring Your Content

Headings organize content and improve readability and SEO.

- **Adding a Heading Block:** Insert a **Heading** block from the block selector.

- **Heading Levels:** Choose H1 to H6 tags. Typically, H1 is reserved for the main title; use H2 for section titles and H3 for subsections.

- **Formatting:** Align and color options available.

Tips:

- Use headings consistently to create a clear content hierarchy.

- Avoid skipping heading levels to maintain structure.

Image Block: Visual Storytelling

Images enhance engagement and illustrate your points.

- **Adding an Image Block:** Select **Image** block and upload or choose from the Media Library.

- **Settings:** Add alt text for accessibility and SEO.

- **Alignment:** Set image alignment and size.

- **Link Settings:** Link the image to a media file, attachment page, or custom URL.

Tips:

- Optimize images for the web (small file size without quality loss).

- Use descriptive alt text for screen readers and SEO.

List Block: Organizing Information

Lists help present information clearly and succinctly.

- **Adding a List Block:** Choose **List** block.
- **Types:** Toggle between bulleted and numbered lists.
- **Indentation:** Create nested lists for subpoints.
- **Formatting:** Basic text formatting and alignment available.

Tips:

- Use lists to break complex information into digestible points.
- Avoid overusing lists to maintain flow.

Quote Block: Highlighting Important Text

Quotes draw attention to impactful statements or citations.

- **Adding a Quote Block:** Select **Quote** block.
- **Styling:** Choose between standard or large styles.
- **Attribution:** Add citation or author name.
- **Formatting:** Basic text options and alignment.

Tips:

- Use sparingly to emphasize key messages.
- Combine with pull quotes in page builders for advanced design.

Combining Blocks: Creating Dynamic Layouts

Blocks can be rearranged by dragging or using arrow controls to adjust content flow. Grouping blocks together or using columns allows for more complex layouts.

Keyboard Shortcuts and Efficiency Tips

- **/ (Slash) Command:** Type / then the block name to quickly insert blocks.
- **Duplicate Blocks:** Select block and press **Ctrl + Shift + D**.
- **Move Blocks:** Use arrow keys or drag-and-drop.
- **Convert Blocks:** Switch between paragraph, heading, list, etc., without deleting content.

Best Practices for Block Editor Use

- Preview your content regularly.
- Use reusable blocks for repeated content like call-to-action buttons.
- Keep your content accessible — use alt text, headings, and clear language.
- Don't overload pages with too many block types to maintain performance.

Practical Exercise: Create a Sample Post

- Add a heading introducing your topic.
- Write a paragraph summarizing it.
- Insert an image related to your content.
- Create a bulleted list of key points.
- Add a relevant quote.
- Preview and publish your post.

Mastering the WordPress Block Editor is essential to creating vibrant, engaging websites in 2025. Its intuitive modular design empowers beginners to craft professional layouts with ease.

Advanced Blocks: Unlocking Creative Flexibility

The WordPress Block Editor breaks the mold of traditional, linear content creation. With advanced blocks, you can organize information visually, guide user actions, and integrate multimedia seamlessly.

Columns Block: Crafting Multi-Column Layouts

The **Columns block** allows you to divide your page or post into side-by-side sections — a key technique for modern, responsive web design.

How to Use Columns

- Add a **Columns block** by clicking the + icon and searching for "Columns."
- Select the number of columns (typically 2 to 4).
- Insert other blocks — paragraphs, images, buttons — into each column.
- Adjust the width of each column by dragging column borders or using block settings.

Benefits of Columns

- **Improves Readability:** Breaks up long text and adds white space.
- **Showcases Comparisons:** Display features, pros and cons, or testimonials side-by-side.
- **Visual Appeal:** Creates dynamic, magazine-style layouts.

Responsive Considerations

WordPress automatically stacks columns vertically on smaller screens, ensuring mobile friendliness. Always preview your page on various devices.

Buttons Block: Driving Visitor Actions

Buttons are essential for directing visitors toward important actions like signing up, purchasing, or contacting you.

Adding and Customizing Buttons

- Insert the **Buttons block** and click **Add Button**.
- Customize the button text and link URL.
- Adjust alignment (left, center, right).
- Choose button style, color, and size from block settings.
- Add multiple buttons side-by-side if needed.

Best Practices for Buttons

- Use clear, action-oriented text (e.g., "Subscribe Now," "Get Started").
- Ensure buttons contrast with the background for visibility.
- Don't overwhelm visitors — use buttons sparingly and strategically.

Media & Text Block: Blending Content and Visuals

The **Media & Text block** pairs an image or video alongside text, ideal for storytelling and product descriptions.

How to Use Media & Text

- Add the **Media & Text block**.
- Upload or select media on one side.
- Write your text on the other.
- Choose the media position (left or right).
- Adjust vertical alignment and content width.

Why Media & Text Works

- Creates balanced, professional-looking sections.
- Maintains alignment and responsiveness automatically.
- Engages users by combining visual and textual information effectively.

Embed Block: Integrating External Content

The **Embed block** lets you insert content from various platforms directly into your page or post.

Supported Embeds

- YouTube videos
- Twitter tweets
- Instagram posts
- Facebook posts
- Spotify playlists
- Vimeo videos
- Google Maps
- And many more.

How to Embed

- Add an **Embed block** or use the shortcut by pasting a URL directly into a paragraph block.

- WordPress automatically converts it into the embedded content.

- Adjust alignment and size settings where available.

Benefits of Embedding

- Enriches your content with multimedia.
- Keeps visitors engaged without leaving your site.
- Adds credibility through social proof.

Creating Beautiful Pages and Posts with Layouts and Design Tips

The magic of the Block Editor lies in the ability to mix and match blocks into compelling, visually appealing layouts. Beyond just inserting blocks, thoughtful design enhances usability and elevates your brand.

Planning Your Layout

Start with your wireframe or sketch (covered in Chapter 2). Define:

- The primary message or goal for the page/post.
- The logical flow from introduction to conclusion.
- Key sections that need visual emphasis.

Using White Space Effectively

White space, or negative space, is the empty area around content.

- Enhances readability.
- Prevents clutter and overwhelm.
- Guides the eye naturally through content.

Avoid packing every inch of the page with text or images. Use spacer blocks or padding controls within blocks to create breathing room.

Aligning and Grouping Blocks

- Use alignment controls to center or justify content.
- Group related blocks using the **Group block** to move and style them as a single unit.
- Combine text blocks with media blocks in columns or media & text for harmony.

Consistency in Typography and Colors

- Choose no more than 2–3 fonts and stick to them.
- Use your brand colors consistently for headings, links, and buttons.
- Utilize block color settings carefully to maintain a cohesive look.

Accessibility and User Experience

- Use headings properly for screen readers and SEO.
- Ensure sufficient color contrast between text and background.
- Provide alt text for all images.
- Avoid using color alone to convey information.

Leveraging Reusable Blocks

For repeated content like call-to-actions, disclaimers, or author bios, create **Reusable Blocks**.

- Save time by reusing content across multiple pages.
- Update once, and all instances update automatically.

Preview and Testing

- Always preview your layout on desktop, tablet, and mobile views.
- Test links, buttons, and embedded content.
- Solicit feedback from peers or users.

Practical Exercise: Build a Sample Landing Page

1. Create a heading introducing a product or service.
2. Add a paragraph summarizing benefits.
3. Insert a two-column layout: an image on the left, text on the right.
4. Add a button block with a clear call-to-action.
5. Embed a related video or testimonial.
6. Include a quote block highlighting customer praise.
7. Preview on different devices and adjust spacing.

Mastering advanced blocks like Columns, Buttons, Media & Text, and Embed turns your material from plain text and photos into dynamic, engaging web pages. When coupled with deliberate design concepts and layout methods, the WordPress Block Editor empowers you to construct professional, beautiful websites without coding.

Reusable Blocks and Templates: Saving Time and Ensuring Consistency

As your website expands, efficiency and consistency become crucial. Repeating the same content pieces across several pages or posts can be tiresome and error-prone. WordPress's Block Editor provides elegant answers to these difficulties through Reusable Blocks and Templates.

What Are Reusable Blocks?

A Reusable Block is a saved group of blocks that you can put several times across your website. When you update the reusable block, all instances reflect those changes instantly.

Imagine you have a call-to-action (CTA) button with a certain style and URL that displays on dozens of pages. Instead of modifying each page manually, you edit the Reusable Block once, and all your CTAs update immediately.

Creating and Using Reusable Blocks

1. **Select the block or group of blocks** you want to reuse.
2. Click on the three-dot menu (block options) in the toolbar.
3. Choose **"Add to Reusable Blocks"**.
4. Name your block clearly, e.g., "Main CTA Button."
5. Save the block.

To use a reusable block:

- Click the + icon to add a block.
- Search for your reusable block by name.
- Insert it wherever needed.

Managing Reusable Blocks

- Edit a reusable block by selecting it in any post or page and clicking **Edit**.
- Or manage all reusable blocks from **Manage All Reusable Blocks** under the block inserter.
- Delete or rename blocks as needed.

Advantages of Reusable Blocks

- **Consistency:** Maintain uniformity in design and messaging.
- **Efficiency:** Save time when creating or updating content.
- **Error Reduction:** Minimize inconsistencies or outdated information.

What Are Templates?

Templates are predefined page or post layouts consisting of multiple blocks arranged in specific structures. While reusable blocks are individual elements, templates represent entire page designs.

Using Templates in WordPress

- WordPress themes may provide built-in templates for pages like "About," "Contact," or "Landing Page."

- The Full Site Editing (FSE) capabilities introduced in recent WordPress versions allow site-wide templates controlling headers, footers, and more.

- Some plugins offer template libraries for rapid page building.

Templates speed up content creation by providing a ready-made framework that you customize.

Creating Custom Templates

Advanced users can create and save custom templates using the Block Editor or tools like the **Reusable Blocks Extended** plugin. These templates can then be applied to new pages or posts, ensuring design uniformity.

Troubleshooting Common Block Editor Issues

Despite its many benefits, users sometimes face challenges with the Block Editor. Recognizing and resolving these issues ensures a smooth content creation experience.

Slow Performance or Lagging

- **Cause:** Large pages with many blocks, conflicting plugins, or low hosting resources.

- **Solution:**

    - Break large content into smaller pages.
    - Disable unnecessary plugins.
    - Upgrade hosting if necessary.

- Clear browser cache and try different browsers.

Blocks Not Loading or Displaying Correctly

- **Cause:** Plugin or theme conflicts, outdated WordPress version.

- **Solution:**

    - Update WordPress, themes, and plugins.
    - Temporarily deactivate plugins to identify conflicts.
    - Switch to a default theme (like Twenty Twenty-Five) to test.

Unable to Add Certain Blocks

- **Cause:** Some plugins restrict specific blocks or custom blocks might not be registered.

- **Solution:**

    - Check plugin settings.
    - Install missing block plugins if needed.
    - Clear cache and reload editor.

Content Disappearing or Not Saving

- **Cause:** JavaScript errors, server timeouts, or security plugins blocking actions.

- **Solution:**

    - Disable browser extensions.
    - Increase server PHP limits.
    - Check security plugin logs and whitelist necessary requests.

Image Upload or Media Issues

- **Cause:** Incorrect file permissions or PHP configuration.

- **Solution:**

    - Ensure media folder permissions are set correctly.
    - Increase upload file size limits in php.ini or hosting panel.

White Screen or Editor Crashes

- **Cause:** Plugin/theme conflicts or corrupted files.
- **Solution:**
    - Enable debugging mode.
    - Replace corrupted files.
    - Restore from backup if needed.

Alternatives and Page Builders: When and Why to Use Them

While Gutenberg is powerful and evolving, some users seek alternatives for specific needs. Page builders are popular plugins that offer drag-and-drop visual editing beyond Gutenberg's native capabilities.

Popular Page Builders

- **Elementor:** Offers extensive design control and a wide array of widgets.
- **Beaver Builder:** Known for reliability and beginner-friendliness.
- **Divi Builder:** Part of the Divi theme, with a strong focus on visual design.
- **WPBakery:** Integrated with many premium themes, offering frontend/backend editing.

Why Consider a Page Builder?

- **Advanced Design Freedom:** Drag-and-drop with pixel-perfect control.
- **Custom Layouts:** More complex grids, animations, and effects.
- **Pre-built Templates:** Ready-made designs for rapid development.
- **Integration:** Often supports third-party add-ons for extended functionality.

When Gutenberg is Enough

- You prefer lightweight, fast-loading websites.
- You want to avoid plugin bloat and potential conflicts.
- You require simple to moderately complex layouts.
- You favor using the latest WordPress features and native tools.

Combining Gutenberg and Page Builders

Some sites benefit from using Gutenberg for standard posts and page builders for landing pages or specialized content. Evaluate based on your needs and testing.

Potential Downsides of Page Builders

- Can increase site load times.
- Sometimes cause lock-in — difficult to switch away later.
- Additional cost for premium versions.
- Steeper learning curve.

Practical Exercise: Create and Manage a Reusable Block and Explore Troubleshooting

- Create a reusable CTA block.
- Insert it in multiple posts.
- Edit the reusable block and observe changes.
- Simulate common issues by disabling plugins and observing effects.
- Explore alternative editors and compare interfaces.

Mastering reusable blocks and templates streamlines your workflow and keeps your content consistent. Being prepared for common Block Editor problems ensures ongoing productivity. While page builders offer sophisticated design possibilities, Gutenberg remains a solid, dynamic core editor that fulfills most purposes quickly.

With these tools and skills, you are enabled to develop appealing, professional content and layouts, building a strong basis for your WordPress site's success.

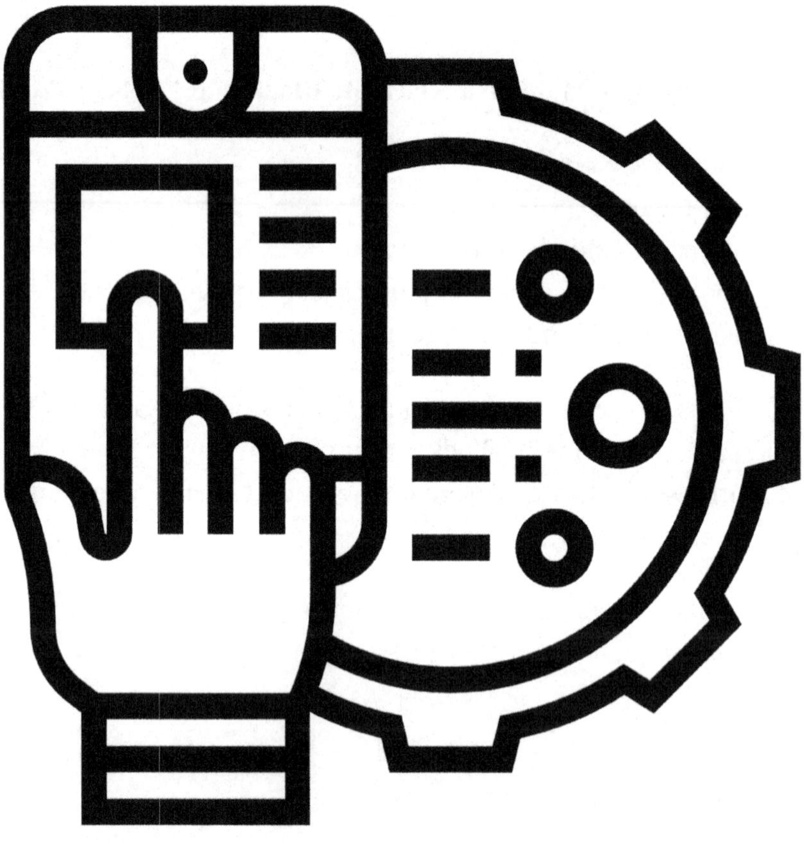

Chapter 5

Selecting and Customizing Themes Like a Pro

Did you know that roughly 94% of first impressions of a website are design-related? Visitors automatically rate your site's authenticity and quality based on how it looks and functions. Selecting the proper WordPress theme is therefore one of the most critical decisions you'll make while constructing your website. The theme determines not just your site's appearance but also its responsiveness, performance, SEO-friendliness, and user experience.

In 2025, with thousands of themes accessible — from free options to expensive marketplaces — understanding how to choose and tweak a theme like an expert may save you time, increase your website's performance, and please your visitors.

This chapter takes you through the essentials of WordPress themes, discusses the distinctions between free and paid options, and educates you on selecting a fast, SEO-friendly, and responsive theme perfectly suited for your site.

Understanding WordPress Themes: Free vs Premium

At its core, a WordPress theme controls the visual design and layout of your website. It dictates how your information is presented: the font, color schemes, header styles, page templates, navigation menus, and much more.

What Are Free Themes?

Free themes are accessible at no cost in the official WordPress theme directory. They offer basic design and customization tools ideal for simple websites.

Advantages of Free Themes:

- **Cost:** Ideal for beginners and tight budgets.
- **Simplicity:** Typically straightforward with fewer complex options.
- **WordPress.org Review:** Themes in the directory undergo quality and security checks.
- **Community Support:** Popular free themes have active user bases.

Limitations of Free Themes:

- **Limited Features:** Fewer customization options and design variations.
- **Basic Support:** Rely mostly on community forums or documentation.
- **Generic Design:** May be widely used, leading to less uniqueness.
- **Performance:** Some free themes may lack optimization, affecting speed.

What Are Premium Themes?

Premium themes are paid themes available through marketplaces like ThemeForest, Elegant Themes, or directly from developers. They typically offer advanced features, customization tools, and dedicated support.

Advantages of Premium Themes:

- **Rich Features:** Advanced layouts, sliders, widgets, and integrations.
- **Customization Options:** Drag-and-drop builders, color pickers, and font selectors.
- **Regular Updates:** Ongoing development to ensure compatibility and security.
- **Professional Support:** Access to support teams or forums.
- **Unique Designs:** More polished and varied aesthetics.

Considerations When Choosing Premium Themes:

- **Cost:** One-time or annual fees ranging from $30 to $100+.
- **Complexity:** Might have a learning curve due to many features.
- **Compatibility:** Ensure compatibility with WordPress versions and plugins.

How to Choose Between Free and Premium Themes?

Your choice depends on:

- **Budget:** Free themes are great for getting started; premium for advanced needs.
- **Functionality:** Complex websites might require premium theme features.
- **Design Preferences:** Premium themes often provide more polished looks.
- **Support Needs:** If you want guaranteed support, premium themes are better.
- **Performance Concerns:** Check theme demos and reviews for speed and responsiveness.

How to Choose a Fast, SEO-Friendly, and Responsive Theme

Selecting a theme isn't just about looks — it impacts your site's performance, search rankings, and visitor experience.

Speed and Performance

Website speed affects user satisfaction and SEO rankings. Slow-loading sites risk losing visitors and falling in search results.

Key Speed Factors in Themes:

- **Lightweight Code:** Avoid themes bloated with unnecessary scripts and styles.
- **Optimized Assets:** Efficient use of images, fonts, and scripts.
- **Minimal External Requests:** Fewer external fonts or scripts reduce loading times.
- **Compatibility with Caching:** Works well with caching plugins to speed up load times.

Testing Speed Before Choosing:

- Visit the theme demo on mobile and desktop.
- Use tools like **Google PageSpeed Insights**, **GTmetrix**, or **Pingdom** to assess performance.
- Check user reviews for comments on speed.

SEO-Friendliness

A theme optimized for SEO helps search engines crawl and rank your site effectively.

SEO Features to Look For:

- **Clean, Semantic Code:** Proper use of HTML5 tags like <header>, <nav>, <main>, <footer>.

- **Schema Markup Support:** Helps search engines understand content context.

- **Fast Load Times:** Speed indirectly impacts SEO.

- **Mobile-Optimized:** Google uses mobile-first indexing.

- **Compatible with SEO Plugins:** Should work seamlessly with tools like Yoast SEO or Rank Math.

- **Accessibility:** Supports screen readers and keyboard navigation, which can affect SEO and user experience.

Responsiveness and Mobile Optimization

More than half of all web traffic comes from mobile devices. Your theme must deliver an excellent experience on smartphones and tablets.

How to Verify Responsiveness:

- Use browser developer tools to simulate different screen sizes.
- Visit the theme demo on multiple devices.
- Look for features like touch-friendly menus and readable fonts on small screens.

Additional Theme Selection Criteria

- **Regular Updates:** Themes should be updated frequently for security and compatibility.

- **Compatibility:** Check that the theme supports the latest WordPress version and popular plugins.

- **Customization Ease:** Look for themes with intuitive customization panels or integration with the WordPress Customizer.

- **Demo Content Availability:** Helpful for beginners to quickly replicate layouts.

- **Translation and Multilingual Ready:** Supports WPML or Polylang plugins if you plan multilingual content.

Customizing Your Theme Like a Pro

Once you've chosen a theme, customization shapes your site's unique identity.

Using the WordPress Customizer

The Customizer offers a live preview of changes as you make them.

Common Customization Options:

- **Site Identity:** Upload logo, site title, and tagline.
- **Colors:** Change background, text, link, and button colors.
- **Typography:** Adjust font types, sizes, and weights.
- **Header and Footer:** Modify layouts, add widgets, or change content.
- **Menus:** Create and assign menus to different locations.
- **Homepage Settings:** Choose a static homepage or latest posts.

Using Theme Options Panels

Premium themes often include their own options panel with more settings such as:

- Layout choices (boxed, full-width).
- Sidebar positions.
- Slider settings.
- Social media integrations.

Using Page Builders with Themes

Some themes are built specifically to work with popular page builders like Elementor or Beaver Builder, giving you drag-and-drop layout control.

Best Practices for Customization

- **Backup Before Changes:** Use backup plugins before major customizations.

- **Use Child Themes:** For advanced CSS or PHP modifications, use child themes to preserve updates.

- **Keep It Simple:** Don't overload with colors or fonts; maintain readability.

- **Test Across Devices:** Ensure your customizations look good on mobile and desktop.

- **Optimize Images:** Use compressed images for faster load times.

Practical Exercise: Selecting and Customizing Your Theme

- Research and shortlist 3 themes matching your site's purpose.
- Test their demos on speed and responsiveness.
- Install a theme and explore the Customizer.

- Upload a logo and adjust colors to fit your brand.
- Set up menus and homepage settings.
- Experiment with widgets and footer customization.

Choosing the correct theme establishes the framework for your website's look, feel, and performance. Whether free or paid, your theme should be quick, SEO-friendly, and responsive to provide visitors with a smooth experience.

Customization brings your distinctive brand to life, allowing your site to stand out and deliver your message successfully.

Installing and Activating Themes: Step-by-Step

Getting the perfect theme starts with learning how to install and activate it correctly. WordPress makes this process uncomplicated, whether you're selecting a free theme from the official directory or uploading a premium theme.

Installing Themes from the WordPress Repository

The easiest way to install a theme is directly from the WordPress Dashboard:

1. **Log into your WordPress Admin Dashboard** by going to www.yoursite.com/wp-admin and entering your credentials.

2. **Access the Themes page:** On the left sidebar, click **Appearance > Themes**.

3. **Add New Theme:** Click the **Add New** button at the top.

4. **Search or Browse Themes:** Use the search bar to find themes by name or filter by features, layout, and popularity.

5. **Preview Themes:** Hover over a theme and click **Preview** to see how it looks on a demo site.

6. **Install Theme:** When you find the perfect theme, click **Install**.

7. **Activate Theme:** Once installed, click **Activate** to make it live on your site.

Uploading Premium or Third-Party Themes

If you purchased or downloaded a theme outside of the WordPress directory, install it manually:

1. **Download the theme ZIP file** from your provider.
2. **In your WordPress Dashboard, go to Appearance > Themes > Add New.**
3. **Click Upload Theme** at the top.
4. **Choose the ZIP file** from your computer and click **Install Now**.
5. **Activate the theme** after installation completes.

After Activation: Initial Theme Setup

Many themes come with setup wizards or demo content imports to help replicate the demo look. Follow theme-specific instructions carefully for best results.

Using the WordPress Customizer: Colors, Fonts, Layouts, and More

The WordPress Customizer is your live design studio. It lets you see changes in real-time as you tweak your site's appearance.

Opening the Customizer

Go to **Appearance > Customize** in your dashboard. A panel appears on the left, and your website preview is on the right.

Core Customization Areas

Site Identity

- **Site Title and Tagline:** Set your website's name and slogan.
- **Site Icon (Favicon):** Upload the small icon shown in browser tabs.

Colors

- Adjust background, header, link, and accent colors.
- Choose colors consistent with your brand to evoke the right emotions.

Typography

- Select fonts for headings, body text, and menus.
- Adjust font sizes, weights, and line heights.
- Use Google Fonts integration for variety.

Layouts

- Configure page width and content area sizes.
- Choose sidebar placement or full-width layouts.
- Some themes offer multiple header and footer layouts.

Menus

- Create, edit, and assign menus to locations like header or footer.
- Add pages, categories, and custom links.

Widgets

- Manage sidebar and footer widgets
- Add text, search bars, recent posts, and more.

Homepage Settings

- Choose to display the latest posts or a static page.
- Assign the front page and posts page accordingly.

Advanced Customizer Features

Some themes add extra options:

- **Header and Footer Editors:** Upload logos, adjust social icons, and add call-to-action buttons.

- **Custom CSS:** Add your own CSS snippets for precise styling.

- **Background Images:** Set images with options for fixed or scrolling behavior.

- **Animations and Effects:** Control transitions, parallax scrolling, and hover effects.

Tips for Effective Customization

- **Consistency is Key:** Use a coherent color palette and font scheme.
- **Test on Devices:** Use preview modes to ensure mobile-friendliness.

- **Don't Overdo It:** Keep designs clean and user-friendly.
- **Save Regularly:** Preview and publish updates carefully.

Child Themes: Why They Matter and How to Create One

When you customize your theme's files directly, those changes are overwritten every time the theme updates. This is where child themes become indispensable.

What Is a Child Theme?

A child theme inherits all the functionality and styling of a parent theme but allows you to override specific files safely. Updates to the parent theme won't erase your customizations.

Why Use a Child Theme?

- **Preserve Customizations:** Keep your changes intact during theme updates.
- **Experiment Safely:** Try new designs or code without breaking the site.
- **Organize Custom Work:** Separate custom CSS, templates, and functions.

How to Create a Child Theme: Step-by-Step

1. **Create a New Folder:** In your WordPress themes directory (wp-content/themes), create a folder named parenttheme-child (replace parenttheme with your theme's name).

2. **Create style.css File:** Inside this folder, create a style.css file with the following header:

css
Copy
```
/*
Theme Name:   Parent Theme Child
Template:     parenttheme
Version:      1.0.0
*/
```

3. **Enqueue Parent Styles:** Create a functions.php file in the child theme folder with PHP code to load the parent theme's styles:

php
Copy
```
<?php
```

82

```php
function child_theme_enqueue_styles() {
    wp_enqueue_style( 'parent-style', get_template_directory_uri() . '/style.css' );
}
add_action( 'wp_enqueue_scripts', 'child_theme_enqueue_styles' );
?>
```

4. **Activate Child Theme:** Go to **Appearance > Themes** and activate your child theme.

Customizing with Child Themes

- Override template files by copying them from the parent theme to the child folder and editing.
- Add custom CSS in the child theme's style.css.
- Add custom PHP functions in the child theme's functions.php.

Plugins for Child Themes

Plugins like **Child Theme Configurator** simplify creating and managing child themes for beginners.

Practical Exercise: Install and Customize a Theme with a Child Theme

- Install a theme of your choice.
- Customize colors and fonts using the Customizer.
- Create and activate a child theme.
- Add custom CSS in the child theme to change a color or font.
- Test your site before and after activating the child theme.

Selecting and tweaking themes with skill guarantees your website shines out while working smoothly. Installing themes properly, using the WordPress Customizer, and employing child themes secure your work and provide unlimited creativity.

Popular Theme Recommendations for Different Website Types in 2025

Themes are built with varying goals, layouts, and features based on the website's purpose. Let's study the top themes recommended for various categories to assist you to the best fit.

83

1. Business and Corporate Websites

Professionalism, clean design, and conversion focus are paramount.

- **Astra:** Lightweight, fast, and highly customizable. Compatible with all major page builders and offers pre-built business templates.
- **GeneratePress:** Performance-focused with modular customization; great for fast-loading corporate sites.
- **OceanWP:** Feature-rich with demos for consulting, finance, and agency websites.
- **Neve:** Modern, mobile-first, and integrates seamlessly with WooCommerce and Elementor.

2. E-Commerce and Online Stores

Smooth shopping experience and product showcase matter.

- **Flatsome:** Designed for WooCommerce, with beautiful product grids and live page building.
- **Shopkeeper:** Elegant, conversion-optimized, with extensive e-commerce functionalities.
- **Porto:** Multi-purpose but excels in e-commerce with fast loading and versatile layouts.
- **Storefront:** Official WooCommerce theme with minimal design and reliable updates.

3. Blogging and Personal Websites

Focus on readability, simplicity, and storytelling.

- **Writee:** Clean typography with customizable layouts suitable for bloggers.
- **Hemingway:** Minimalist and distraction-free, ideal for writers and journalists.
- **Kadence:** Flexible and lightweight, with blog-specific customization options.
- **Baskerville:** Beautiful grid layouts and featured post options.

4. Portfolio and Creative Sites

Visual presentation and artistic flair take center stage.

- **Uncode:** Highly customizable with a strong focus on creative portfolios.
- **Oshine:** Offers over 50 demos and powerful visual editing for creatives.
- **Kalium:** Perfect for photographers, designers, and artists with portfolio-focused features.
- **Flox:** Minimal and modern, emphasizing large images and clean typography.

5. Nonprofit and Charity Websites

Highlight mission and encourage donations clearly.

- **Charity Foundation:** Purpose-built for nonprofits with donation integration.
- **Benevolent:** Clean design with volunteer and event management features.
- **GivingPress Lite:** Free, straightforward, and donation-friendly.
- **Alone:** Beautiful design for causes and campaigns with CTA focus.

6. Educational Websites and Online Courses

Organize information and present learning materials clearly.

- **Education WP:** Built for LMS with lesson management and quizzes.
- **Eduma:** Comprehensive educational theme with LearnPress integration.
- **LMS:** Focuses on course sales and student engagement.
- **Academy:** Clean design with course lists, instructor profiles, and reviews.

How to Choose the Right Theme for You

- Align theme demos with your content type.
- Prioritize speed and mobile responsiveness.
- Check for recent updates and good reviews.
- Ensure compatibility with essential plugins.

Fixing Common Theme Issues and Compatibility Tips

Even the best themes can bring issues, especially as WordPress and plugins evolve. Being prepared to recognize and fix common issues protects your site from downtime and unpleasant user experiences.

Common Theme Issues

1. Theme Conflicts with Plugins

- **Symptoms:** Features not working, broken layouts, JavaScript errors.

- **Solution:**

    - Deactivate all plugins and reactivate one by one to identify conflicts.

- Check plugin and theme documentation for compatibility notes.
- Update both theme and plugins to latest versions.

2. Slow Loading Times

- **Symptoms:** Pages take too long to load, user bounce rates increase.

- **Solution:**

    - Use a lightweight theme optimized for performance.
    - Optimize images and enable caching plugins.
    - Minimize the use of heavy slider plugins or animations.

3. Responsive Design Issues

- **Symptoms:** Site looks broken or elements overlap on mobile.

- **Solution:**

    - Test with multiple devices and adjust CSS if needed.
    - Use the WordPress Customizer's mobile preview.
    - Contact theme support if bugs persist.

4. Styling or Layout Broken After Updates

- **Symptoms:** Unexpected visual glitches after theme or WordPress update.

- **Solution:**

    - Use a child theme for customizations.
    - Clear caching plugins and browser cache.
    - Review changelogs for theme updates to identify breaking changes.

Compatibility Tips

- **Always Backup:** Before updating themes or plugins, backup your site.

- **Test Updates on a Staging Site:** Prevent issues on live sites by testing updates in a safe environment.

- **Choose Well-Maintained Themes:** Prioritize themes with frequent updates and active support.

- **Limit the Number of Plugins:** Fewer plugins reduce compatibility issues.

- **Keep WordPress Core Updated:** Run the latest version for security and compatibility.

- **Check Browser Compatibility:** Verify site appearance across major browsers.

When to Seek Support or Consider Changing Themes

- If persistent issues remain unresolved by updates or fixes.
- When themes don't support necessary features.
- If performance cannot be improved.
- When support forums or developers are unresponsive.

Practical Exercise: Evaluate and Troubleshoot a Theme

- Select a theme and install it on a test site.
- Activate key plugins and observe any issues.
- Use developer tools to inspect console errors.
- Try fixing conflicts by disabling plugins.
- Review theme update notes for known issues.

Choosing a theme matched to your website's purpose, backed by thoughtful consideration of performance and compatibility, lays the scene for success. Coupled with preparedness to recognize and address typical theme difficulties, you maintain a seamless and engaging user experience.

By mastering theme selection and debugging, you develop confidence to personalize and optimize your WordPress site like an expert – ready to delight visitors and meet your goals in 2025 and beyond.

Chapter 6

Essential Plugins for Every Website

WordPress's core software is excellent, but its true charm rests in its extensibility through plugins. As of 2025, the official WordPress Plugin Directory has over 60,000 plugins, ranging from simple contact forms to full-fledged e-commerce systems. This huge ecosystem allows website owners to add feature, better security, improve performance, and personalize their sites to their individual needs - without writing a single word of code.

In reality, research suggests that the average WordPress site utilizes between 10 to 20 plugins to maintain optimal performance and user experience. Understanding what plugins are, why they matter, and how to safely identify, install, and activate them is important to constructing a successful website.

This chapter will lead you through the essentials of plugins, how to traverse the plugin ecosystem safely, and highlight must-have plugins for every site.

What Are Plugins and Why They Matter

At its essence, a plugin is a piece of software that "plugs into" your WordPress site to offer new capabilities or enhance existing functionality. Think of WordPress as the engine of a car, and plugins as accessories that modify and enrich the ride.

Why Plugins Are Important

- **Expand Functionality:** Add contact forms, SEO tools, social sharing buttons, galleries, sliders, and more.

- **Improve Security:** Use security plugins that monitor and protect your site from threats.

- **Boost Performance:** Caching and optimization plugins improve load times.

- **Simplify Management:** Automate backups, analytics, and spam control.

- **Enhance User Experience:** Add membership systems, forums, e-commerce capabilities.

- **Save Time and Money:** Avoid custom coding by leveraging existing solutions.

Without plugins, WordPress would be a powerful but basic CMS. With plugins, it becomes infinitely adaptable.

Types of Plugins You Might Need

- **Security:** Protect against hacks and malware.
- **SEO:** Optimize content for search engines.
- **Performance:** Speed up your site.
- **Backup:** Schedule and manage backups.
- **E-commerce:** Sell products and services.
- **Social Media:** Enable sharing and social login.
- **Analytics:** Track visitor behavior.
- **Forms:** Create contact, survey, or registration forms.
- **Spam Protection:** Filter unwanted comments and messages.

How to Find, Install, and Activate Plugins Safely

While plugins provide enormous value, irresponsible installation might introduce dangers such as security vulnerabilities, performance degradation, or site conflicts. Knowing how to safely pick and manage plugins is vital.

Finding Plugins Safely

Use the Official WordPress Plugin Directory

The safest place to find plugins is the official repository at wordpress.org/plugins. These plugins are reviewed for code quality and security.

- Browse categories or search by name or function.
- Check ratings, number of active installations, and last updated date.
- Read reviews to gauge user satisfaction.

Trusted Premium Marketplaces

Premium plugins often offer advanced features and support.

- Purchase from reputable sources like CodeCanyon, Elegant Themes, or directly from developers.

- Verify refund policies and update frequency.

Avoid Untrusted Sources

Never download plugins from unverified sites or torrents. These can contain malware.

Installing Plugins: Step-by-Step

1. **Log into your WordPress Dashboard.**
2. Go to **Plugins > Add New**.
3. Search for the plugin by name or functionality.
4. Review plugin details, ratings, and compatibility.
5. Click **Install Now**.
6. Once installed, click **Activate**.

Uploading Premium or Custom Plugins

If you have a plugin file (.zip):

1. In **Plugins > Add New**, click **Upload Plugin**.
2. Select the plugin ZIP file.
3. Click **Install Now**.
4. Activate the plugin.

Activating Plugins

Activation makes the plugin functional on your site. After activation.

- Some plugins require configuration through their own settings pages.
- Others work automatically upon activation.

Managing Plugins Safely

- **Update Regularly:** Keep plugins updated to patch security holes and bugs.
- **Deactivate and Delete Unused Plugins:** Inactive plugins can still pose risks.
- **Test New Plugins on Staging Sites:** Avoid conflicts and downtime.
- **Backup Before Major Changes:** Protect your data before installing or updating.

Signs of Unsafe or Problematic Plugins

- Rarely or never updated.
- Poor or no support.
- Low user ratings.

- Known security vulnerabilities reported online.
- Conflicts causing site errors or slowdowns.

Must-Have Plugins for Every Website

While your needs may vary, the following categories and examples represent essential plugins to get started.

Security Plugins

- **Wordfence Security:** Firewall, malware scanner, login protection.
- **Sucuri Security:** Security activity auditing, malware scanning.
- **iThemes Security:** Brute force protection and security hardening.

SEO Plugins

- **Yoast SEO:** Guides optimization of posts, generates sitemaps.
- **Rank Math:** Advanced SEO features, rich snippet support.
- **All in One SEO Pack:** Comprehensive SEO toolkit.

Performance and Caching Plugins

- **WP Rocket:** Caching, minification, lazy loading.
- **W3 Total Cache:** Improves server performance and caching.
- **Autoptimize:** Aggregates and optimizes scripts and styles.

Backup Plugins

- **UpdraftPlus:** Automated backups to cloud storage.
- **BackupBuddy:** Scheduled backups and restores.
- **BackWPup:** Full backups and database optimization.

Contact Forms

- **WPForms:** Drag-and-drop form builder.
- **Contact Form 7:** Popular, flexible free form plugin.
- **Ninja Forms:** User-friendly form creation.

Spam Protection

- **Akismet:** Filters spam comments effectively.
- **Antispam Bee:** Lightweight and effective spam filter.

Analytics and Tracking

- **MonsterInsights:** Google Analytics integration.
- **ExactMetrics:** User-friendly analytics reporting.

Social Sharing and Integration

- **Social Warfare:** Customizable share buttons.
- **AddToAny:** Supports multiple social networks.
- **Revive Old Posts:** Automatically shares content on social media.

Practical Exercise: Safely Installing and Configuring Essential Plugins

- Install and activate a security plugin and configure basic firewall settings.
- Set up an SEO plugin and optimize your homepage meta description.
- Install a caching plugin and test your site speed.
- Create a contact form using a drag-and-drop builder.
- Schedule your first automated backup.

Plugins increase your WordPress website's capabilities, making it flexible to practically any purpose. However, the power of plugins comes with responsibility – selecting, installing, and managing them correctly ensures your site remains secure, fast, and reliable.

Must-Have Plugins for SEO, Security, Speed, and Backups

WordPress core is powerful, but crucial site characteristics like SEO optimization, protection against attacks, fast loading, and reliable backups come from the proper plugins.

SEO Plugins: Boosting Your Site's Visibility

Search Engine Optimization (SEO) is crucial for getting organic visitors. Without it, your material may never reach the eyes of potential visitors.

Top SEO Plugins in 2025

- **Yoast SEO:** The most popular SEO plugin, Yoast offers on-page optimization, XML sitemaps, readability analysis, and meta tag management.

- **Rank Math:** Known for an intuitive interface and powerful features including schema markup, keyword tracking, and integration with Google Search Console.

- **All in One SEO Pack:** Comprehensive SEO toolkit ideal for beginners and advanced users alike.

What SEO Plugins Do

- Help optimize titles, meta descriptions, and URLs.
- Generate sitemaps to help search engines crawl your site.
- Analyze readability and keyword density.
- Manage redirects and canonical URLs.
- Integrate with social media previews.

Security Plugins: Shielding Your Website

With WordPress powering nearly 43% of the web, it's a prime target for hackers. Security plugins defend your site against malware, brute-force attacks, and vulnerabilities.

Recommended Security Plugins

- **Wordfence Security:** Combines firewall, malware scanning, login security, and live traffic monitoring.

- **Sucuri Security:** Provides comprehensive auditing, malware detection, and post-hack cleanup services.

- **iThemes Security:** Offers over 30 ways to secure your site including two-factor authentication, strong password enforcement, and database backups.

Key Security Features to Look For

- Web Application Firewall (WAF).
- Real-time malware scanning.
- Login protection and brute force attack prevention.
- Two-factor authentication (2FA).

- Security activity auditing and notifications.

Speed and Performance Plugins: Fast Websites Win

Speed impacts user experience and search rankings. Slow sites lose visitors and conversions.

Leading Performance Plugins

- **WP Rocket:** A premium caching plugin with easy setup, file minification, lazy loading, and database cleanup.

- **W3 Total Cache:** Free, comprehensive caching and CDN integration plugin.

- **Autoptimize:** Focuses on optimizing scripts, styles, and HTML to improve load times.

How Speed Plugins Help

- Cache static versions of pages to reduce server load.
- Minify CSS, JavaScript, and HTML files.
- Enable lazy loading of images and videos.
- Integrate with Content Delivery Networks (CDNs).
- Clean up database overhead.

Backup Plugins: Your Safety Net

Unexpected issues—hacking, server crashes, or user errors—can damage your site. Regular backups ensure you can restore your site quickly.

Popular Backup Plugins

- **UpdraftPlus:** Easy-to-use, schedules automated backups to remote locations like Dropbox or Google Drive.

- **BackupBuddy:** Paid plugin with full-site backups, scheduled restores, and migration features.

- **BackWPup:** Free, supports multiple cloud storage options and database optimization.

Backup Best Practices

- Schedule daily or weekly backups depending on update frequency.
- Store backups off-site, separate from your server.
- Test backup restoration to ensure data integrity.

Plugins for Enhancing User Experience: Contact Forms, Social Sharing, Analytics

Your website's success depends on engagement. Plugins that facilitate communication, sharing, and understanding visitor behavior are essential.

Contact Form Plugins

Simple, secure, and customizable contact forms help visitors reach you easily.

- **WPForms:** Drag-and-drop form builder with templates for contact, surveys, payments.
- **Contact Form 7:** Lightweight, flexible, and widely supported.
- **Ninja Forms:** User-friendly and extendable with add-ons.

Social Sharing Plugins

Encourage visitors to share your content, increasing reach and traffic.

- **Social Warfare:** Attractive share buttons with customization options.
- **AddToAny:** Supports over 100 social networks and includes share counters.
- **Monarch:** Elegant sharing and follow buttons from Elegant Themes.

Analytics Plugins

Tracking visitor behavior helps you refine content and marketing strategies.

- **MonsterInsights:** Simplifies Google Analytics integration with dashboards inside WordPress.

- **ExactMetrics:** Real-time stats, event tracking, and audience insights.

- **Google Site Kit:** Official Google plugin combining Analytics, Search Console, AdSense, and PageSpeed Insights.

Managing Plugin Updates and Compatibility Checks

Plugins evolve. Regular updates patch vulnerabilities, add features, and improve compatibility. But unmanaged updates can cause conflicts.

Best Practices for Plugin Management

- **Backup First:** Always backup your site before updating.
- **Test Updates on Staging:** Safely test updates before applying them live.
- **Update Regularly:** Keep plugins current to avoid security risks.
- **Deactivate and Delete Unused Plugins:** Reduce bloat and attack surfaces.
- **Monitor Site Post-Update:** Check key functionality and site performance.
- **Use Compatible Plugins:** Confirm plugins support your WordPress and PHP versions.

Troubleshooting Plugin Conflicts

- Identify conflicts by deactivating plugins one by one.
- Resolve issues by updating or replacing problematic plugins.
- Consult plugin support forums for developers.
- Consider using health check plugins to diagnose issues.

Practical Exercise: Plugin Setup and Management Workflow

- Install and configure a security plugin and run an initial scan.
- Set up an SEO plugin and optimize your homepage.
- Install a caching plugin and measure speed improvements.
- Create a contact form and embed it on your contact page.
- Connect Google Analytics using a plugin.
- Schedule plugin updates and backup routines.

Plugins are the heartbeat of your WordPress website, expanding capabilities far beyond the basic system. Carefully picked, well-managed plugins optimize SEO, protect your site, speed up performance, and improve user interaction. By understanding plugin fundamentals and update practices, you develop a comprehensive, engaging, and high-performing website set for growth.

Avoiding Plugin Conflicts and Performance Issues

When numerous plugins are running, occasionally they can conflict with each other or with your theme, producing problems like broken layouts, errors, or poor loading times. Understanding how to prevent and fix these conflicts is vital for a healthy WordPress site.

Understanding Plugin Conflicts

Plugin conflicts occur when two or more plugins seek to use the same resources, functions, or scripts in incompatible ways. Common symptoms include:

- White screen of death.
- Missing features or buttons.
- Layouts breaking or pages not displaying correctly.
- Error messages on the frontend or backend.
- Slow site performance or timeouts.

Common Causes of Conflicts

- Plugins that duplicate functionality.
- Outdated plugins incompatible with current WordPress version.
- Plugins that use conflicting JavaScript or CSS libraries.
- Poorly coded plugins not following WordPress standards.
- Theme and plugin compatibility issues.

Best Practices to Avoid Plugin Conflicts

1. Research Before Installing

- Choose well-reviewed plugins with a large user base.
- Check the last update date — prefer actively maintained plugins.
- Read compatibility notes and user feedback.

2. Limit the Number of Plugins

- Avoid installing plugins that offer overlapping features.
- Consolidate features when possible (e.g., use one SEO plugin instead of multiple).

3. Test on a Staging Site

- Before activating new plugins on your live site, test them in a staging environment.
- Verify all key site features and forms work properly.

4. Update Regularly

- Keep WordPress core, themes, and plugins up to date.
- Updates often include bug fixes and compatibility improvements.

5. Backup Before Changes

- Always backup your site before installing, updating, or deleting plugins.

Diagnosing and Fixing Conflicts

Step 1: Identify the Problem

- Use the **Health Check & Troubleshooting** plugin to safely test plugin conflicts by disabling all plugins and enabling them one by one in troubleshooting mode.

- Manually deactivate all plugins and reactivate one at a time to pinpoint the conflicting plugin.

Step 2: Resolve or Replace

- Contact plugin support for help.
- Search for alternative plugins that provide similar features without conflicts.
- Update or rollback to a previous plugin version if needed.

Performance Issues Caused by Plugins

Too many or poorly optimized plugins can drastically slow your website.

How to Prevent Plugin-Related Performance Issues

- Use lightweight, efficient plugins known for good performance.
- Avoid plugins that load heavy scripts on every page if not necessary.
- Monitor site speed regularly using tools like Google PageSpeed Insights or GTmetrix.
- Use caching and optimization plugins to mitigate load.
- Disable or remove plugins not in use.

Step-by-Step Guide to Building Custom Functionality Without Coding

Want to add unique features without hiring a developer or learning code? WordPress's ecosystem offers tools and techniques that let you build custom functionality visually and intuitively.

Using Page Builders to Add Custom Layouts and Features

Popular drag-and-drop page builders enable you to create advanced layouts with buttons, forms, galleries, sliders, and more:

- **Elementor:** Offers extensive widgets, popup builders, and theme builder functionality.
- **Beaver Builder:** Known for stability and user-friendly interface.
- **Divi Builder:** Integrated with Divi theme, with advanced design options.

These builders allow you to:

- Design custom headers, footers, and pages.
- Insert dynamic content like testimonials, pricing tables, countdown timers.
- Integrate forms and calls to action seamlessly.

Using Plugin-Based Custom Functionality Builders

Some plugins offer visual tools to create forms, custom post types, or workflows:

- **WPForms:** Drag-and-drop form builder for contact, surveys, payments.
- **Advanced Custom Fields (ACF):** Add custom fields to posts/pages visually.
- **Toolset:** Create custom post types, fields, and relationships without code.
- **AutomatorWP:** Automate workflows based on user actions.

Using Shortcodes and Widgets

- Many plugins provide **shortcodes** — snippets you insert into pages or posts that generate dynamic content like galleries, buttons, or user profiles.

- WordPress **widgets** let you place blocks of content into sidebars, footers, or other widget-ready areas without coding.

Using the Block Editor for Custom Functionality

The WordPress Block Editor itself supports advanced blocks and reusable blocks to build complex features:

- Create custom block layouts with Columns, Media & Text, Buttons.

- Use third-party block collections like **Stackable** or **Ultimate Addons for Gutenberg** for extra features.

- Save complex block groups as reusable blocks for use across your site.

Integrating Third-Party Services Without Code

- Embed email opt-in forms from services like Mailchimp or ConvertKit using provided embed codes.

- Use social media embed blocks to integrate Instagram, Twitter, or YouTube.

- Connect Google Analytics or Facebook Pixel via plugins or scripts added through plugins like **Insert Headers and Footers**.

Practical Exercise: Add a Custom Contact Form and Call to Action

1. Install a form builder plugin like WPForms.
2. Use the drag-and-drop interface to create a contact form.
3. Add the form block or shortcode to a page.
4. Insert a styled button using the Block Editor.
5. Link the button to your contact page or newsletter signup.
6. Test the form submission.

Using Code Snippets Without Full Plugin Installation

For small customizations, the **Code Snippets** plugin lets you add PHP snippets safely without editing theme files or creating plugins.

Understanding how to avoid plugin conflicts and manage performance issues preserves your site's health and stability. At the same time, new WordPress tools let you add custom features and layouts without writing code, opening unlimited possibilities for your website's growth.

Mastering these concepts ensures your WordPress site remains adaptable, secure, and personalized to your particular vision.

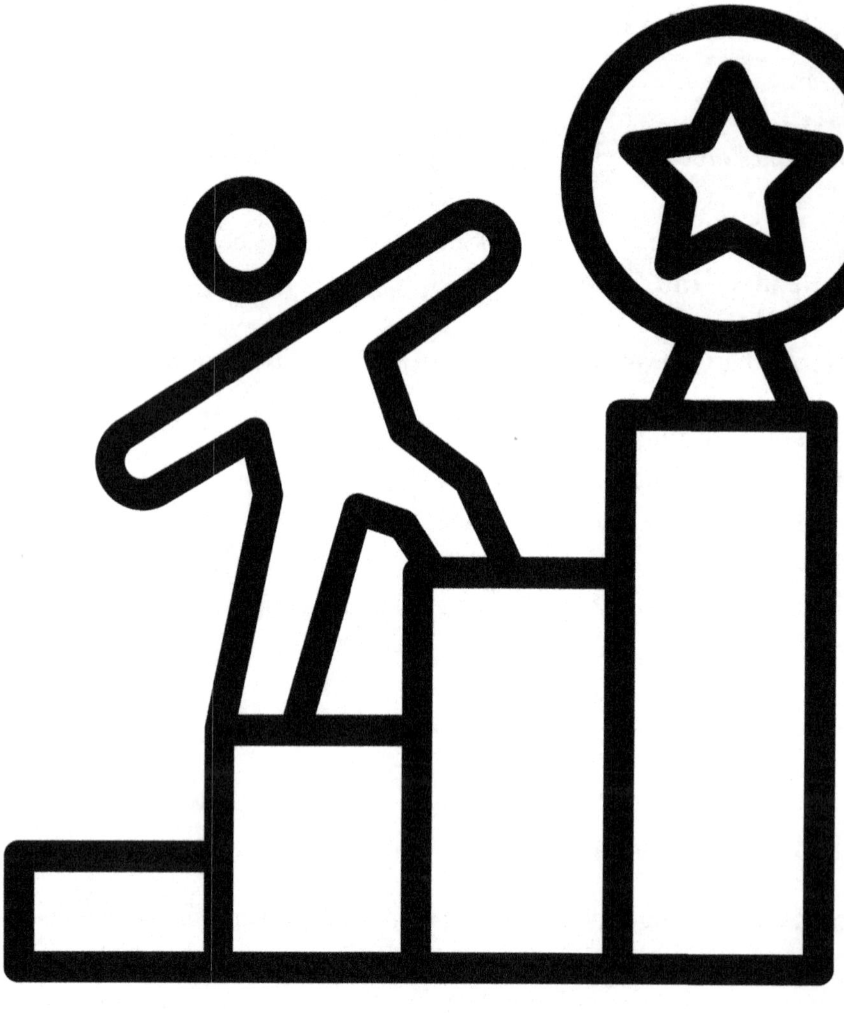

Chapter 7

Creating and Managing Content Effectively

Did you know that websites with well-organized content see up to 40% higher visitor engagement and longer session durations? Publishing outstanding material is just the start. How you organize and present that content can either welcome your visitors or leave them confused and frustrated.

WordPress, as a content management system, gives flexible tools to produce and organize information effectively. Understanding the major differences between Posts and Pages, and using Categories and Tags effectively, enables you to construct a website that's easy to explore, search-engine friendly, and personalized to your audience's needs.

This chapter will lead you through the essentials of content kinds in WordPress and practical ways for arranging your site's content efficiently.

The Difference Between Posts and Pages — When to Use Each

WordPress categorizes material largely into two types: Posts and Pages. While they may look similar during design, they have quite different purposes on your site.

What Are Posts?

Posts are dynamic items that provide the backbone of blogs, news sites, and often updated material. They are designed to be timely and appear in reverse chronological order on your blog or news feed.

Key Features of Posts:

- **Time-sensitive:** Posts usually reflect current events, announcements, or regular updates.
- **Categorized and Tagged:** You can organize posts with categories and tags.
- **Social Sharing:** Typically shareable and linked through RSS feeds
- **Author and Date:** Display author info and publication dates.
- **Comments:** Often enabled to encourage discussion.
- **Archive:** Posts are archived by date, category, or tag.

102

What Are Pages?

Pages are static, timeless content not meant for frequent updates. They are foundational to your website's structure.

Key Features of Pages:

- **Static Content:** Ideal for evergreen information like About Us, Contact, Services.
- **Hierarchy:** Pages can have parent and child pages, allowing nested structures.
- **No Categories or Tags:** Pages aren't organized with categories or tags.
- **No Time Stamps:** Pages do not show publication dates or authors.
- **Comments:** Usually disabled.

When to Use Posts

- Publishing blog articles or news.
- Sharing tutorials, opinions, or stories.
- Creating event announcements or press releases.
- Posting updates or newsletters.

When to Use Pages

- About your business or website.
- Contact information and forms.
- Privacy policy, terms, and legal disclaimers.
- Service descriptions and FAQs.
- Landing pages or sales pages.

Hybrid Use Cases

Some websites blur the lines between posts and pages, but generally:

- Use posts to keep your content fresh and engaging.
- Use pages to provide stable, important information.

Organizing Content with Categories and Tags

When your site grows, organizing content becomes essential for user experience and SEO. WordPress's **Categories** and **Tags** system is a powerful way to classify and structure your posts.

Categories: The Broad Topics

Categories group posts into broad topics or themes. They help users find related content easily.

- Each post must have at least one category.
- Categories can be hierarchical, allowing subcategories.
- Categories appear in menus, archives, and widgets.
- Example: For a food blog, categories might be "Recipes," "Reviews," "Nutrition."

Tags: The Specific Details

Tags describe specific details or keywords related to a post.

- They are non-hierarchical.
- A post can have many tags.
- Tags help users find posts with similar topics or terms.
- Example: In a recipe post, tags might be "vegan," "gluten-free," "dessert."

Best Practices for Categories and Tags

- **Use Categories Sparingly:** Limit categories to a handful of broad topics.
- **Use Tags Liberally:** Add relevant, specific tags to enhance content discoverability.
- **Be Consistent:** Use a consistent naming convention to avoid duplicates or confusion.
- **Avoid Over-tagging:** Don't overload posts with irrelevant tags.
- **Use SEO Tools:** Plugins like Yoast SEO help manage categories and tags effectively.

How Categories and Tags Help Visitors

- Improve **user experience** by grouping related content.
- Enable better **site navigation** and reduce bounce rates.
- Enhance **internal linking**, which benefits SEO.
- Facilitate **archive pages** where users can explore similar topics.

Creating and Managing Posts and Pages

Creating a Post

1. Go to **Posts > Add New**.
2. Enter your title and write your content using the Block Editor.
3. Assign categories and tags on the right sidebar.
4. Set a featured image if applicable.

5. Preview and publish when ready.

Creating a Page

1. Go to **Pages** > **Add New**.
2. Add a title and content.
3. Organize pages by setting parent pages if needed.
4. Preview and publish.

Editing and Organizing Content

- Use the **All Posts** or **All Pages** screen to manage, edit, or delete content.
- Bulk actions let you categorize or trash multiple posts.
- Use **Quick Edit** for fast metadata changes.

Tips for Effective Content Management

- Plan your categories before launching the site.
- Use **menus** to highlight important pages.
- Utilize **widgets** like category lists or tag clouds for sidebar navigation.
- Regularly audit your categories and tags to remove redundancies.
- Leverage **custom taxonomies** for specialized classification if needed.

Practical Exercise: Organize Your Content

- Create 3 pages (About, Contact, Services).
- Write 5 posts assigned to at least two categories.
- Add relevant tags to each post.
- Build a menu including your pages and category links.
- Use a widget to display categories in the sidebar.

Effective content development goes hand-in-hand with clever organization. Understanding whether to use posts versus pages, and leveraging the power of categories and tags, allows you to develop a website that is intuitive for visitors and optimized for search engines. This foundation not only enhances your site's usability but sets you up for long-term growth and engagement.

Best Practices for Writing SEO-Friendly Content in 2025

SEO — or Search Engine Optimization — is the process of tailoring your content to rank well in search engines like Google. With algorithms evolving to reward quality and user experience, SEO in 2025 demands a smart, balanced strategy.

Understand User Intent

Today's SEO revolves around meeting the intent behind search queries. Whether users want to learn, buy, compare, or be entertained, your content should satisfy those needs.

- **Informational:** Provide clear, detailed answers.
- **Transactional:** Guide users toward purchases or actions.
- **Navigational:** Help users find specific information or sites.

Keyword Research and Placement

Keywords remain essential but should be used naturally.

- Use tools like **Google Keyword Planner**, **Ubersuggest**, or **Ahrefs** to identify relevant keywords.

- Focus on long-tail keywords that reflect specific queries.

- Place keywords in:

    - Title tags.
    - Headers (H1, H2).
    - Meta descriptions.
    - Opening paragraphs.
    - Image alt text.

Avoid keyword stuffing — write for people first.

Write Engaging, Readable Content

- Use clear, concise language.
- Break text into short paragraphs.
- Use bullet points and numbered lists.
- Employ headings to organize sections.
- Incorporate storytelling or examples to engage readers.

Optimize Meta Descriptions and Titles

Your meta title and description appear in search results — make them compelling to increase click-through rates.

- Keep titles under 60 characters.
- Meta descriptions around 150-160 characters.

- Include target keywords naturally.

Use Structured Data and Schema Markup

Schema helps search engines understand content context, enabling rich results.

- Use plugins like **Yoast SEO** or **Schema Pro**.

- Add markup for articles, products, reviews, events, FAQs.

Ensure Mobile-Friendliness and Fast Load Times

Google prioritizes mobile-first indexing.

- Use responsive themes.
- Optimize images and media.
- Minimize heavy scripts and third-party embeds.

Update Content Regularly

Keep posts fresh by updating statistics, links, and adding new insights.

Adding Images, Videos, and Other Media Correctly

Multimedia enhances engagement, explains concepts visually, and breaks up text, making content more digestible.

Adding Images

- Upload images via **Media Library** or directly into posts/pages.

- Use high-quality, relevant images.

- Compress images for faster loading using tools like **TinyPNG** or plugins like **Smush**.

- Add **Alt Text** describing the image for accessibility and SEO.

- Use appropriate file formats: JPEG for photos, PNG for graphics with transparency, SVG for logos and icons.

Adding Videos

Videos boost time-on-site and engagement.

- Upload videos to platforms like **YouTube** or **Vimeo** — avoid uploading large video files directly.

- Use the WordPress **Embed block** or paste video URLs to auto-generate embedded players.

- Add captions or transcripts to improve accessibility.

- Optimize video titles and descriptions for SEO.

Other Media Types

- **Audio:** Podcasts or music can be embedded similarly.
- **Documents:** PDFs or presentations can be linked or embedded.
- **Interactive Content:** Forms, polls, or quizzes engage users.

Best Practices for Media Usage

- Ensure media relevance and quality.
- Use consistent styling and sizing.
- Provide captions or descriptions when needed.
- Test media on various devices and browsers.

Using Galleries, Sliders, and Featured Images

Visual presentation impacts how users perceive and interact with your content.

Galleries

Create galleries to showcase multiple images attractively.

- Use the WordPress **Gallery block** to insert image grids.

- Customize columns, cropping, and linking options.

- Use plugins like **Envira Gallery** or **NextGEN Gallery** for advanced features like lightboxes or filters.

Sliders

Sliders display images or content slides sequentially and can highlight promotions or portfolios.

- Choose lightweight slider plugins like **Smart Slider 3** or **MetaSlider**.
- Avoid auto-play sliders that move too fast, frustrating users.
- Ensure sliders are responsive and accessible.

Featured Images

A featured image represents your post or page visually.

- Upload a compelling featured image for every post.
- Use consistent image dimensions for visual harmony.
- Featured images often appear in post previews, social shares, and widgets.

Combining Visual Elements for Impact

- Balance text and images to avoid clutter.
- Use whitespace effectively.
- Align images with content flow.
- Use captions to provide context.

Practical Exercise: Create a Rich Media Post

- Write a post with a clear headline and subheadings.
- Insert a relevant featured image.
- Add multiple images using the Gallery block.
- Embed a YouTube video related to your content
- Optimize all media with alt text and captions.
- Preview your post on desktop and mobile.

Effective content development in 2025 goes beyond words. SEO-friendly language mixed with thoughtful use of photos, videos, and interactive media captivates visitors and boosts your site's performance on search engines. Galleries, sliders, and featured photos boost the visual experience, making your material engaging and memorable.

Scheduling Posts and Managing Content Calendar

Scheduling lets you post content automatically at certain dates and times, ensuring your website never stays silent—even while you're busy.

Why Scheduling Matters

- **Consistent Publishing:** Builds trust with your audience and search engines.
- **Time Management:** Allows batching content creation and timed releases.
- **Global Reach:** Publish at optimal times for different time zones.
- **Marketing Strategy:** Coordinates content with campaigns, holidays, or events.

Scheduling Posts in WordPress: Step-by-Step

WordPress has built-in scheduling capabilities:

1. **Create Your Post:** Go to **Posts > Add New** and write your content.

2. **Set the Publish Date:**

    - In the right sidebar under **Post Settings**, find the **Publish** section.
    - Click the date and time next to **Publish immediately**.
    - Choose your desired future date and time.

3. **Click Schedule:** WordPress will queue the post to go live at that moment.

4. **Manage Scheduled Posts:** Under **Posts > All Posts**, scheduled posts appear with the status "Scheduled" and the publish date.

Managing Your Content Calendar

For greater control and visibility, content calendar plugins provide drag-and-drop interfaces and collaboration features.

Popular Content Calendar Plugins

- **Editorial Calendar:** A free, simple drag-and-drop calendar showing scheduled and drafted posts.

- **CoSchedule:** Premium plugin combining social media scheduling and content calendar.

- **PublishPress:** Includes editorial calendar, notifications, and permissions.

- **WP Scheduled Posts:** Manages scheduling and auto-publishing with content calendar visualization.

Benefits of Using a Content Calendar

- Visualize your posting schedule.
- Plan thematic content or series.
- Coordinate with team members or guest writers.
- Avoid content gaps or clustering.
- Track deadlines and editorial workflow.

Best Practices for Scheduling and Calendars

- Plan content weeks or months ahead.
- Balance evergreen and timely content.
- Use consistent posting frequency.
- Monitor analytics to adjust publishing times.
- Integrate calendar with marketing and social platforms.

Editing and Updating Content Without Breaking Your Site

Maintaining accurate, up-to-date content is essential but carries risks if done carelessly. Changes can break layouts, cause errors, or harm SEO if URLs or metadata are altered improperly.

Best Practices for Safe Content Updates

1. Backup Before Major Changes

Use backup plugins like **UpdraftPlus** or **BackupBuddy** to create full backups before editing critical posts or pages.

2. Use the Block Editor's Preview Feature

Before publishing updates, use the **Preview** button to check how changes look on different devices and browsers.

3. Avoid Changing URLs (Permalinks) Unnecessarily

Changing post or page URLs can break links and hurt SEO. If you must change a permalink:

- Set up 301 redirects to the new URL using plugins like **Redirection**.
- Update internal links accordingly.

4. Update Metadata Carefully

Maintain or improve SEO titles, descriptions, and schema data using SEO plugins without deleting important metadata.

5. Edit in Small Steps

Break large edits into smaller updates to monitor their impact.

6. Use Staging Sites for Complex Updates

For major redesigns or content overhauls, use a staging environment to test changes without affecting your live site.

Editing Posts and Pages: Step-by-Step

1. Go to **Posts** > **All Posts** or **Pages** > **All Pages**.
2. Hover over the item and click **Edit**.
3. Make your changes using the Block Editor.
4. Click **Preview** to review.
5. Click **Update** to publish changes.

Monitoring and Quality Control

- Use **Revision History** in WordPress to compare versions and restore earlier drafts if needed.
- Enable spell-checking and grammar tools like **Grammarly**.
- Audit images and media to ensure they remain relevant and optimized.
- Check page load speed after changes.

Handling Comments and User-Generated Content

- Moderate comments to prevent spam and maintain community quality.
- Respond promptly to engage your audience.
- Use plugins like **Akismet** to filter spam comments.

Keeping Content Fresh and Relevant

- Schedule content reviews quarterly or biannually.
- Update statistics, links, and references regularly.
- Refresh images and videos to maintain appeal.

Practical Exercise: Schedule and Update Content:

- Write and schedule five posts with staggered publish dates.
- Edit one published post by adding new information and updating images.
- Preview and test changes before publishing.
- Use a content calendar plugin to visualize your schedule.

Creating and managing content properly is the engine that fuels your website's growth. Scheduling provides consistency and purposeful publishing, while careful editing preserves your site's quality and trustworthiness.

By mastering these abilities, you develop a trustworthy, engaging platform that people return to and search engines reward.

Chapter 8

Website Navigation and User Experience (UX)

Did you know that approximately 70% of people decide whether to stay or leave a website within only seconds — and a complicated navigation layout is one of the top reasons they leave? Effective website navigation is more than a function; it's a vital pillar of user experience (UX) that directly affects engagement, conversions, and brand perception.

In 2025, with the rise of mobile browsing and varied devices, creating clear, intuitive menus and well-structured navigation systems has never been more crucial. Alongside menus, footer and sidebar widgets provide significant locations to expand your site's functionality and accessibility without overwhelming the main content area.

This chapter unpacks established ways for building menus and navigation systems that help users locate what they need effortlessly. It also covers how to employ footer and sidebar widgets to increase usability and add value.

Designing Clear Menus and Navigation Structures

Menus are the fundamental roadmap of your website. A well-designed menu lets visitors navigate your information naturally and quickly.

Understanding Menu Types in WordPress

- **Primary Menu:** Usually at the top of the site, guiding main navigation.

- **Secondary Menu:** Often smaller, placed above or below primary menus, or in the header.

- **Footer Menu:** Located at the bottom, provides links to less prominent but important pages.

- **Mobile Menu:** Adapted for small screens, typically collapsible or hamburger style.

Principles of Effective Menu Design

1. Keep It Simple and Focused

Limit menu items to 5-7 top-level links. Too many choices overwhelm users.

2. Use Clear, Descriptive Labels

Menu labels should communicate the content they lead to plainly — avoid jargon or creative but vague wording.

3. Prioritize Important Pages

Place your most visited or conversion-focused pages in the primary menu.

4. Maintain Consistency

Keep menu location and style consistent across pages for familiarity.

5. Use Hierarchical Menus Sparingly

Dropdowns and submenus help organize, but too many levels can confuse visitors.

Planning Your Navigation Structure

Start by mapping out your site's content and grouping related pages. Create categories or sections that users expect. Common menu structures include:

- Home | About | Services | Blog | Contact

- Home | Shop | Categories | Cart | Account

Consider user goals and business objectives to determine menu priorities.

Creating Menus in WordPress: Step-by-Step

1. Go to **Appearance** > **Menus** in your dashboard.
2. Click **Create New Menu**, name it (e.g., Primary Menu).
3. Add pages, categories, or custom links to your menu.
4. Drag and drop items to reorder or create submenus by indenting.
5. Assign the menu to a location defined by your theme.
6. Save your menu.

Optimizing Menus for Mobile Users

- Use responsive menus that collapse into hamburger icons.
- Ensure touch-friendly targets.
- Avoid large dropdowns difficult to interact with on small screens.

Enhancing Menus with Mega Menus

For content-rich sites, **mega menus** display many links in organized panels.

- Use plugins like **Max Mega Menu** to create advanced menus.
- Group related links with headings and columns.
- Include images or icons for better recognition.

Creating Footer and Sidebar Widgets

Widgets are blocks of content you place in widget-ready areas like footers and sidebars. They complement main content and improve navigation and engagement.

What Are Widgets?

Widgets can display:

- Recent posts
- Search bars
- Contact information
- Social media links
- Calendars
- Custom menus
- Subscription forms

Why Use Footer and Sidebar Widgets?

- **Enhance Accessibility:** Provide quick links and tools.
- **Promote Engagement:** Highlight recent or popular content.
- **Support Conversion:** Add newsletter signups or calls to action.
- **Improve Usability:** Offer search, categories, or archives for easier exploration.

Configuring Widgets in WordPress

1. Go to **Appearance > Widgets**.
2. Identify available widget areas (e.g., Sidebar, Footer Column 1).
3. Drag desired widgets into these areas.
4. Customize widget settings.
5. Save changes and preview on the site.

Best Practices for Widget Use

- **Avoid Clutter:** Limit number of widgets per area.
- **Use Logical Groupings:** Group related functions (e.g., recent posts with categories).
- **Keep Design Cohesive:** Match widget styles with your theme.
- **Test Responsiveness:** Widgets should adapt well to mobile.

Popular Widgets to Consider

- **Search Widget:** Helps visitors quickly find content.
- **Custom Menu Widget:** Adds navigation menus in sidebars or footers.
- **Text Widget:** Display custom messages, HTML, or ads.
- **Social Icons Widget:** Link to social profiles.
- **Newsletter Signup:** Integrate with services like Mailchimp.

Advanced Widget Options

Many themes and plugins add custom widgets for enhanced functionality:

- Display related posts with thumbnails.
- Embed Google Maps or contact info.
- Show Instagram feeds or Twitter timelines.

Practical Exercise: Build Your Website's Navigation and Widget Areas

- Create a primary menu with 5-7 key links.
- Assign menus to theme locations.
- Add widgets to your sidebar: search, recent posts, categories.
- Populate footer widget areas with contact info, social links, and a newsletter signup.
- Test navigation and widgets on mobile devices.

Effective navigation and well-planned widget areas create seamless user experiences that invite exploration and engagement. Clear menus guide visitors naturally through your site, while thoughtfully placed widgets add value and accessibility without overwhelming.

Optimizing Your Site for Mobile Visitors

Mobile optimization is no longer a luxury — it's a requirement. Google's mobile-first indexing means your site's mobile version is the primary basis for ranking and visibility.

Why Mobile Optimization Matters

- **User Expectations:** Visitors expect seamless mobile experiences.
- **SEO Impact:** Google prioritizes mobile-friendly sites in search results.
- **Conversion Rates:** Mobile-optimized sites see higher engagement and conversions.
- **Competitive Advantage:** Many sites still struggle with mobile UX.

Characteristics of a Mobile-Optimized Website

- Responsive design that adjusts layout based on screen size.
- Fast loading times, even on slower mobile networks.
- Touch-friendly elements with adequate spacing.
- Readable text without zooming.
- Accessible menus and navigation.
- Optimized images and media for mobile devices.

How to Optimize Your WordPress Site for Mobile

1. Choose a Responsive Theme

- Select themes designed for mobile-first experiences.
- Test demos on multiple devices.
- Themes like Astra, Neve, and GeneratePress excel in responsiveness.

2. Use the WordPress Customizer's Mobile Preview

- Customize font sizes, colors, and spacing specifically for mobile.
- Adjust header and footer layouts.

3. Optimize Images and Media

- Compress images with plugins like Smush or ShortPixel.
- Use modern formats like WebP.
- Implement lazy loading for images and videos.

4. Simplify Navigation for Mobile

- Use collapsible menus or hamburger icons.
- Ensure clickable elements are large and well-spaced.

5. Minimize Plugin Load

- Remove unnecessary plugins that add scripts slowing mobile load.
- Use performance plugins like WP Rocket with mobile caching.

6. Optimize Fonts and Buttons

- Use legible fonts with minimum sizes (usually 16px or higher).
- Buttons and links should be at least 48x48 pixels for easy tapping.

Testing Mobile Optimization

- Use **Google Mobile-Friendly Test** tool.
- Check your site on multiple real devices.
- Use Chrome Developer Tools to simulate different screen sizes.
- Monitor mobile performance via **PageSpeed Insights**.

Accessibility Basics: Making Your Site Inclusive

Accessibility means designing your website so people with disabilities — visual, auditory, motor, or cognitive — can access and use your content effectively.

Why Accessibility Matters

- Ethical responsibility to include all users.
- Legal requirements in many countries.
- SEO benefits from semantic HTML and proper markup.
- Expands your audience and potential customers.

Core Accessibility Principles

- **Perceivable:** Information and UI must be presentable to users in ways they can perceive.

- **Operable:** Interface components must be operable via keyboard or assistive technologies.

- **Understandable:** Content and operation of UI must be understandable.

- **Robust:** Content must be robust enough to work with current and future assistive technologies.

How to Make Your WordPress Site Accessible

1. Use Accessible Themes

- Choose themes that follow WCAG 2.1 guidelines.
- Themes like Twenty Twenty-One, Astra, and GeneratePress are accessibility-ready.

2. Add Alt Text to Images

- Describe the content or function of images for screen readers.
- Avoid empty alt text except for decorative images.

3. Use Proper Heading Structure

- Use heading tags (H1-H6) sequentially to organize content.
- Avoid skipping heading levels.

4. Ensure Keyboard Accessibility

- All interactive elements (links, buttons, forms) must be usable with keyboard only.

5. Use ARIA Landmarks and Roles

- Plugins like **WP Accessibility** can help add ARIA roles.

6. Provide Sufficient Color Contrast

- Use tools like the WebAIM Contrast Checker.
- Avoid relying on color alone to convey meaning.

7. Caption Videos and Provide Transcripts

- Make multimedia accessible by adding captions and transcripts.

8. Use Accessible Forms

- Label all form fields clearly.
- Group related fields logically.

Testing Accessibility

- Use browser extensions like **Ax Accessibility Checker**.
- Test with screen readers like NVDA or VoiceOver.
- Conduct user testing with people with disabilities.

Adding Search Functionality and Breadcrumbs

Efficient navigation isn't just menus — search boxes and breadcrumbs significantly enhance user experience.

Adding Search Functionality

Search allows users to find specific content quickly.

Built-In WordPress Search

- Use the **Search Widget** to add a search box to sidebars or headers.
- Customize search results page with plugins or theme templates.

Enhanced Search Plugins

- **Relevanssi:** Provides fuzzy matching, keyword highlighting, and custom results.
- **SearchWP:** Premium plugin offering advanced search for custom fields and post types.
- **Ajax Search Lite:** Adds live search suggestions and responsive designs.

Best Practices for Search

- Place the search box prominently.
- Use placeholder text like "Search articles..." to guide users.
- Optimize search results for relevance.

Breadcrumbs: Showing Your Path

Breadcrumbs display the user's location within your site's hierarchy, usually near the top of a page.

Benefits of Breadcrumbs

- Improve usability by helping users backtrack.
- Enhance SEO by clarifying site structure.
- Reduce bounce rates.

Adding Breadcrumbs in WordPress

- Some themes include built-in breadcrumb support.
- Use SEO plugins like **Yoast SEO** or **Rank Math** which offer breadcrumb features.
- Add breadcrumbs manually using plugins like **Breadcrumb NavXT**.

Configuring Breadcrumbs

- Display breadcrumbs near the page title or top menu.
- Use simple, clear labels.
- Avoid overcrowding the interface.

Practical Exercise: Optimize Your Site for Mobile and Accessibility

- Test your site with Google's Mobile-Friendly Test.
- Install and configure an accessibility plugin like WP Accessibility.
- Add and customize a search widget.
- Enable breadcrumbs via Yoast SEO or Breadcrumb NavXT.
- Verify keyboard navigation on your site.

Optimizing your website for mobile visitors, making content accessible for all users, and increasing navigation with search and breadcrumbs are key steps toward a truly user-centered website. These initiatives not only raise engagement and enjoyment but also improve SEO and inclusivity, establishing your website for success in 2025 and beyond.

Speed Optimization Techniques: Caching, Image Compression, and Lazy Loading

Website speed is a vital issue that impacts both SEO and user delight. WordPress, being immensely adaptable, demands deliberate techniques to work at its optimum.

Caching: Delivering Content Faster

Caching makes and saves static copies of your web pages, decreasing server load and expediting page delivery to visitors.

Types of Caching

- **Browser Caching:** Stores site elements in the visitor's browser to avoid reloading on return visits.

- **Page Caching:** Saves static HTML versions of dynamic pages.

- **Object Caching:** Caches database query results to speed up data retrieval.

- **CDN Caching:** Content Delivery Networks cache your content on servers worldwide for faster regional access.

Popular WordPress Caching Plugins

- **WP Rocket:** Easy-to-use, comprehensive caching with file optimization and preload.
- **W3 Total Cache:** Advanced caching options, CDN support.
- **WP Super Cache:** Simple setup, static page caching.
- **LiteSpeed Cache:** Best for LiteSpeed servers but compatible elsewhere.

Setting Up Caching

1. Choose a caching plugin compatible with your hosting.
2. Activate basic page caching and browser caching.
3. Configure advanced options like minification of CSS/JS files.
4. Test your site speed before and after enabling caching.

Image Compression: Reducing File Size Without Losing Quality

Images often constitute the largest portion of page weight, making optimization essential.

Compression Methods

- **Lossy Compression:** Reduces file size by removing some data, slightly lowering quality.
- **Lossless Compression:** Shrinks files without quality loss.

Recommended Plugins for Image Compression

- **Smush:** Automated compression and lazy loading.
- **ShortPixel:** Advanced lossy and lossless options.
- **Imagify:** Optimizes images on upload and bulk compresses.
- **EWWW Image Optimizer:** Supports various formats with CDN integration.

Best Practices

- Use modern formats like WebP for superior compression.
- Resize images to the actual display size.
- Compress images before upload or use plugin automation.

Lazy Loading: Loading Images and Media On-Demand

Lazy loading defers loading of images and videos until they enter the visitor's viewport, reducing initial load time.

Benefits

- Speeds up first meaningful paint.
- Saves bandwidth, especially on mobile devices.
- Improves overall site responsiveness.

How to Enable Lazy Loading

- Use native lazy loading supported by modern browsers by adding the loading="lazy" attribute.

- Use plugins like **Lazy Load by WP Rocket** or **a3 Lazy Load** to implement more advanced lazy loading.

- Check theme compatibility and plugin conflicts.

Testing UX: Tools and Techniques to Improve Visitor Interaction

Speed is only one side of the coin. User experience focuses on how visitors interact with your site — ease of use, engagement, and satisfaction.

Why Test UX?

- Identify usability issues.
- Understand visitor behavior.
- Increase conversions and retention.
- Reduce bounce rates.

Essential UX Testing Tools

1. Heatmaps and Session Recordings

Visualize where visitors click, scroll, and spend time.

- **Hotjar:** Combines heatmaps, visitor recordings, and feedback polls.
- **Crazy Egg:** Offers heatmaps and A/B testing tools.
- **Mouseflow:** Tracks mouse movements and scroll depth.

2. User Testing Platforms

Gather qualitative feedback by watching real users interact.

- **UserTesting:** Provides video feedback from target audience.
- **Lookback:** Allows live interviews and usability testing.
- **UsabilityHub:** Quick preference and navigation tests.

3. Analytics and Behavior Flow

Understand overall user behavior patterns.

- **Google Analytics:** Behavior flow, site speed, bounce rates.
- **Microsoft Clarity:** Free heatmaps and session recordings.

UX Testing Techniques

A/B Testing

Compare two versions of a page to see which performs better.

- Use plugins like **Nelio A/B Testing** or services like Google Optimize.

Mobile Usability Testing

Test your site on multiple devices and screen sizes.

- Use Chrome DevTools device toolbar.
- Test real devices if possible.

Accessibility Testing

Ensure your site is usable by people with disabilities.

- Use tools like **axe Accessibility Scanner** or **WAVE**.

Gathering and Acting on Feedback

- Use surveys and polls to ask visitors about their experience.
- Monitor feedback from social media and support requests.
- Prioritize fixes that address common pain points.

Practical Exercise: Speed and UX Optimization Workflow

1. Install and configure a caching plugin.
2. Compress and optimize images on your site.
3. Enable lazy loading and test page load times.
4. Set up Hotjar or Microsoft Clarity to collect heatmap data.
5. Run an accessibility audit with a browser extension.
6. Collect user feedback via surveys.
7. Analyze results and implement prioritized improvements.

Website speed and user experience are inseparable variables driving your site's success. Employing caching, image optimization, and lazy loading provides speedy performance, while UX testing tools empower you to design intuitive, compelling interactions.

By mastering these tactics, you construct a WordPress website that not only draws visitors but keeps them coming back – a key feat in today's digital landscape.

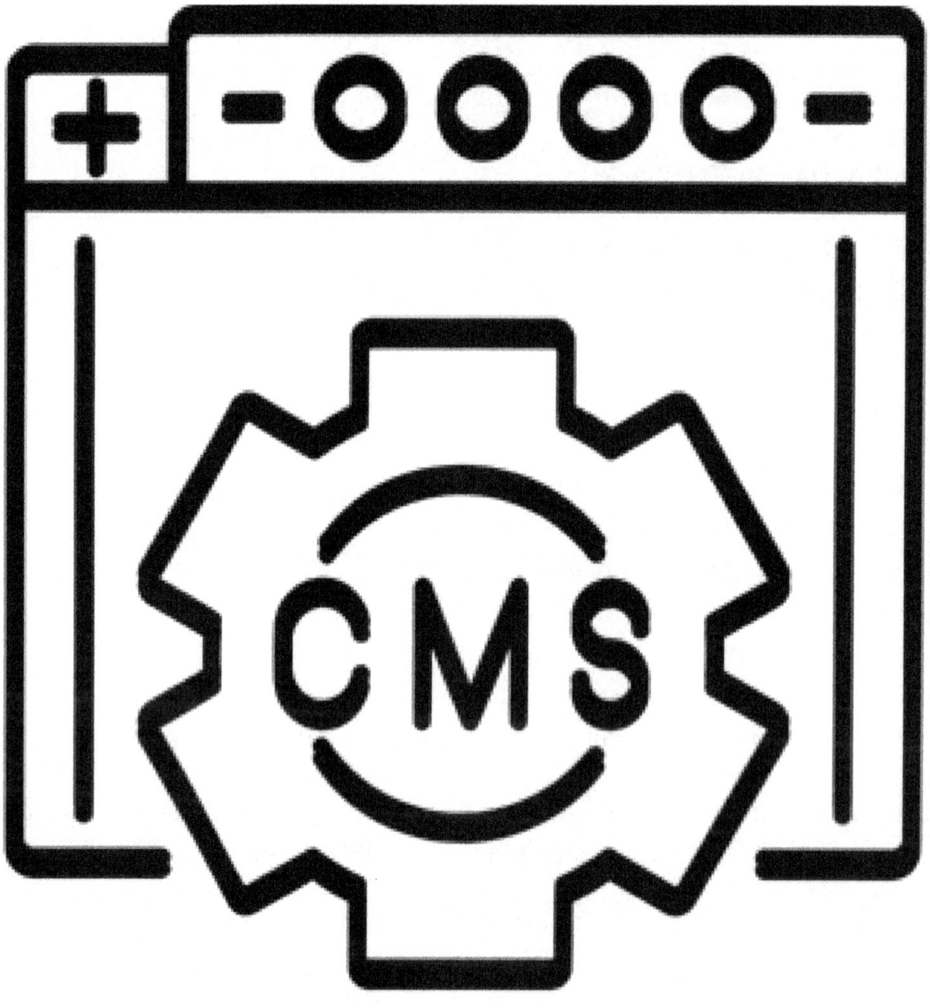
CMS

Chapter 9

Securing Your WordPress Site and Managing Backups

In 2025, WordPress powers roughly 43% of all websites on the internet, making it the most popular content management system in the world. This prominence makes it a favorite target for hackers and other actors. According to recent studies, over 90,000 websites are hacked every day worldwide, many of them are tiny business or personal websites with insufficient security measures in place.

The good news is, safeguarding your WordPress site does not require you to be a cybersecurity specialist. With the correct precautions, you can safeguard your site, your data, and your visitors from typical attacks. Equally vital is having a dependable backup solution in place – so if something does go wrong, you can swiftly restore your site without losing valuable material or functionality.

In this chapter, you will learn how to identify typical security issues WordPress sites face, adopt strong password policies, activate two-factor authentication (2FA), and set up effective backups to keep your website safe and robust.

Understanding WordPress Security Risks and Vulnerabilities

Why WordPress Sites Are Targeted

WordPress's open-source nature allows anyone to contribute to its development, making it adaptable and configurable. However, this openness also means hackers regularly hunt for holes in the core software, themes, plugins, or hosting infrastructures to exploit.

Most WordPress security vulnerabilities occur not from WordPress itself, but from obsolete software, poorly designed themes or plugins, and weak user credentials. Understanding these hazards can help you take effective measures to avert them.

Common Security Threats to WordPress Sites

1. Outdated Core, Themes, and Plugins

WordPress regularly releases updates to patch security holes and improve functionality. When you delay installing these updates, your site becomes vulnerable to known exploits. Many hacks happen because sites run old, unsupported versions of WordPress or plugins.

How to prevent: Always keep WordPress core, themes, and plugins up to date. Enable automatic updates where possible or schedule regular manual updates.

2. Weak Usernames and Passwords

Using predictable usernames like "admin" and simple passwords makes it easy for hackers to gain unauthorized access through brute force attacks (where attackers try multiple username-password combinations).

How to prevent: Use unique usernames and strong, complex passwords. Avoid common words, repeated characters, or simple sequences.

3. Plugin and Theme Vulnerabilities

Plugins and themes add valuable features to your website, but poorly coded or abandoned ones can create security holes. Sometimes vulnerabilities are introduced through third-party plugins, giving hackers a backdoor into your site.

How to prevent: Only install plugins and themes from trusted sources. Remove any unused plugins or themes to minimize risk.

4. SQL Injection and Cross-Site Scripting (XSS)

These are technical attacks where hackers inject malicious code into your website's database or code to steal data or take control.

How to prevent: Use security plugins that scan for suspicious activity and block malicious code. Also, keep your site updated to patch known vulnerabilities.

5. File Inclusion Exploits

Hackers try to upload malicious files or replace legitimate files on your server, allowing them to control your website or server.

How to prevent: Limit file permissions on your server and restrict who can upload files. Regularly scan your website for unexpected files.

Why Regular Security Measures Matter for Beginners

Even if your site is small or new, it is a potential target. Automated bots scan thousands of websites every day looking for weak points. Taking basic security steps early helps you avoid headaches later. Plus, securing your site protects your visitors from phishing scams, malware, or data theft linked to your site.

Implementing Strong Password Policies

Passwords are the first line of defense protecting your WordPress admin area and user accounts. Weak passwords can quickly undo other security efforts.

What Makes a Password Strong?

- **Length:** At least 12 characters is ideal.

- **Complexity:** Mix uppercase and lowercase letters, numbers, and symbols.

- **Unpredictability:** Avoid dictionary words, common phrases, or predictable substitutions like "Pa$$w0rd."

- **Uniqueness:** Use a unique password for your WordPress login, not one you reuse from other sites.

How to Enforce Strong Passwords on Your WordPress Site

WordPress now requires strong passwords for new users, but older accounts or certain user roles might still use weak ones. Here's how to enforce strong passwords and help users create them:

1. **Use a Password Strength Enforcement Plugin:** Plugins like *Force Strong Passwords* or *Password Policy Manager* can require users to create strong passwords when registering or changing passwords.

2. **Educate Users:** If your site has multiple users, communicate password best practices clearly. Encourage the use of password managers to generate and store strong passwords securely.

3. **Regularly Update Passwords:** It's a good habit to update passwords periodically, especially for administrator accounts.

How to Change Your WordPress Password

To update your password safely:

- Log in to your WordPress dashboard.
- Click on **Users** > **Profile**.
- Scroll to **Account Management** and click **Generate Password**.
- WordPress will suggest a strong password, or enter your own.
- Save the changes.

Using Password Managers

Password managers like *LastPass*, *1Password*, or *Bitwarden* securely generate, store, and autofill complex passwords for your accounts. They are invaluable tools to maintain strong, unique passwords without having to remember each one.

Enabling Two-Factor Authentication (2FA)

While strong passwords protect your site, adding a second verification step significantly increases security. This method, known as two-factor authentication, requires users to confirm their identity using a second device or method beyond just the password.

What is Two-Factor Authentication?

Two-factor authentication adds an extra layer of security by requiring two forms of identification:

1. **Something You Know:** Your password.
2. **Something You Have:** A device like your phone or a hardware token.

Even if a hacker obtains your password, they cannot access your account without the second factor.

How 2FA Works on WordPress

After entering your username and password, you'll be prompted to enter a code sent to your phone, generated by an authenticator app, or received via email or SMS. Only after entering this code will you be granted access.

Setting Up 2FA on Your WordPress Site

1. **Choose a 2FA Plugin:**
    Popular free options include *Two Factor Authentication* by David Anderson, *WP 2FA*, or *Google Authenticator* plugins.

2. **Install and Activate the Plugin:**

    - Go to **Plugins > Add New**.
    - Search for the plugin name.
    - Click **Install** and then **Activate**.

3. **Configure the Plugin:**

    - Navigate to the plugin's settings in the dashboard.
    - Choose which user roles will be required to use 2FA (e.g., Admins, Editors).
    - Select your preferred authentication method: authenticator app (recommended), email, SMS, or hardware token.

4. **Set Up Your Authenticator App:**

    - Download an authenticator app like *Google Authenticator*, *Authy*, or *Microsoft Authenticator* on your smartphone.
    - Scan the QR code provided by the plugin during setup.
    - The app will generate time-based codes to enter when logging in.

5. **Test Your 2FA Login:**

    - Log out of WordPress.
    - Attempt to log in again; you should be prompted for a code from your authenticator app.

Tips for Using 2FA Effectively

- **Backup Codes:** Save backup codes provided by the plugin in a secure location. These allow access if you lose your phone.

- **Multiple Authentication Methods:** Some plugins allow setting up alternative methods, like email codes or hardware keys, for flexibility.

- **Educate Other Users:** If your site has multiple users, guide them through setting up their 2FA to protect all accounts.

Benefits of Using 2FA

- Protects against brute force and password theft.
- Secures accounts even if passwords are compromised.
- Adds peace of mind for site owners and users alike.

Protecting Your Website with Firewalls and Anti-Malware Plugins

Every day, millions of websites fall victim to malware outbreaks, hacking attempts, and other cyber dangers. Even modest personal blogs or corporate sites can be attacked, frequently by automated bots hunting for weak places. Malware can damage your site, steal important data, or use your server to launch attacks on others.

One useful defensive layer is the usage of firewalls and anti-malware plugins made expressly for WordPress. These technologies act like security guards, looking over your site to restrict suspicious behavior and detect malicious code.

What Is a Web Application Firewall (WAF)?

A Web Application Firewall, or WAF, operates as a gatekeeper between your website and the internet. It inspects incoming traffic and stops requests that appear harmful before they reach your site. Unlike typical firewalls that defend networks, a WAF focuses on web traffic and protects your site from common threats such as:

- SQL injections
- Cross-site scripting (XSS)
- Brute force login attempts
- Spam comments and bots

By filtering out bad traffic, a WAF can prevent many attacks before they have a chance to cause harm.

Types of Firewalls for WordPress

1. **Cloud-Based Firewalls:**
   These firewalls operate at the server or DNS level, filtering traffic before it even reaches your hosting provider. Examples include services like *Cloudflare* and *Sucuri Firewall*.

They are powerful and effective, especially for high-traffic or business-critical sites.

2. **Plugin-Based Firewalls:**
   Installed directly on your WordPress site as plugins, these firewalls monitor incoming requests and scan for threats in real time. Examples include *Wordfence* and *All In One WP Security & Firewall*. They provide detailed security reports and allow configuration from your dashboard.

How to Set Up a Firewall Plugin on Your WordPress Site

Let's walk through setting up a popular plugin-based firewall: **Wordfence Security**. It's one of the most widely used WordPress security plugins, offering firewall and malware scanning features in one package.

Step 1: Install and Activate Wordfence

- Go to your WordPress dashboard.
- Click **Plugins > Add New**.
- Search for "Wordfence Security."
- Click **Install Now** and then **Activate**.

Step 2: Configure Firewall Settings

- After activation, you will see the Wordfence menu in your dashboard sidebar. Click on it.

- Navigate to **Firewall > Manage Firewall**.

- Wordfence will prompt you to optimize the firewall for better protection by configuring your .htaccess file. Follow the on-screen instructions to enable "Extended Protection" — this ensures the firewall runs before other plugins and WordPress core files.

- You may be asked to enter your email to receive alerts about security events and updates.

Step 3: Set Firewall Mode

- Choose the firewall mode that best fits your site:

    - **Learning Mode:** For the first 1-2 weeks, Wordfence learns your site's traffic patterns and adjusts rules to reduce false positives.

- o **Enabled and Protecting:** After learning, switch to this mode for full protection.

- Keep the firewall enabled and monitor alerts.

Monitoring and Managing Firewall Alerts

- Wordfence provides real-time alerts about blocked IPs, login attempts, and other suspicious activity.

- Regularly check the **Dashboard > Firewall** section to review security status.

- If you notice repeated attacks from certain IP addresses, you can block them permanently under the **Blocking** tab.

Anti-Malware Plugins: What They Do

Anti-malware plugins scan your WordPress files for malicious code, backdoors, or suspicious modifications. They help detect infections early and can sometimes repair or quarantine infected files.

Popular anti-malware plugins for WordPress include:

- **MalCare**
- **Sucuri Security**
- **Wordfence Scanner** (part of Wordfence plugin)
- **Anti-Malware Security and Brute-Force Firewall**

How to Set Up an Anti-Malware Plugin: Example with MalCare

Step 1: Install and Activate MalCare

- From your WordPress dashboard, go to **Plugins > Add New**.
- Search for "MalCare Security."
- Click **Install Now** and **Activate**.

Step 2: Initial Scan

- Once activated, go to **MalCare > Dashboard**.
- Click **Scan Site** to perform a deep malware scan. This process can take a few minutes depending on your site size.
- MalCare uses cloud-based scanning to reduce server load and detect malware accurately.

Step 3: Clean Infected Files

- If malware is detected, MalCare offers an automatic cleanup option (in the premium version).
- Alternatively, the plugin will provide a detailed report of infected files for manual review.

Best Practices for Using Firewall and Anti-Malware Plugins

- **Keep Plugins Updated:** Just like WordPress core, security plugins receive frequent updates to protect against new threats. Always update them promptly.

- **Don't Overload Your Site:** Avoid installing multiple security plugins with overlapping features, as this can cause conflicts and slow your site. Choose comprehensive solutions.

- **Review Logs Regularly:** Monitor security logs to spot unusual activity early.

- **Use Security Plugins Alongside Hosting Security:** Some hosting providers offer server-level firewalls and malware scanning, which complement plugin-based tools.

Configuring Regular Backups: Manual and Automated Methods

Even with the strongest security precautions, no website is 100% immune to failure, hacking, or unintentional data loss. Backups are your safety net. They allow you to restore your entire site — including content, design, and settings — to a previous healthy condition.

What to Back Up on Your WordPress Site

A complete backup should include:

- **WordPress Core Files:** The core WordPress software files.
- **Themes and Plugins:** Your installed themes and plugins with their settings.
- **Uploads:** Media files like images, videos, PDFs — anything uploaded through the media library.
- **Database:** The heart of your site containing posts, pages, comments, users, and settings.

Manual Backup Method

Performing manual backups is a straightforward way to understand what your site consists of, though it can be time-consuming.

Step 1: Backing Up Files via FTP or File Manager

- Access your website files through an FTP client like *FileZilla* or your hosting control panel's file manager.

- Download the entire WordPress directory (usually public_html or www). This includes wp-content (themes, plugins, uploads) and core files.

Step 2: Export the Database

- Access your hosting control panel and open **phpMyAdmin**.
- Select your WordPress database.
- Click **Export**, choose the **Quick** export method, and save the .sql file to your computer.

Advantages and Disadvantages of Manual Backups

- **Advantages:** Full control over your files, no extra cost.
- **Disadvantages:** Time-consuming, requires technical knowledge, easy to forget or make mistakes.

Automated Backup Plugins

Automated plugins simplify the backup process by scheduling regular backups and storing them safely.

Popular WordPress backup plugins include:

- **UpdraftPlus**
- **BackupBuddy**
- **Duplicator**
- **Jetpack Backup**

Setting Up Automated Backups with UpdraftPlus

UpdraftPlus is one of the most popular and beginner-friendly backup plugins available.

Step 1: Install and Activate UpdraftPlus

- From your dashboard, go to **Plugins > Add New**.
- Search for "UpdraftPlus."
- Click **Install Now** and **Activate**.

Step 2: Configure Backup Schedule

- Navigate to **Settings** > **UpdraftPlus Backups**.

- Click **Settings** tab.

- Choose a backup schedule for files and databases. Recommended: Weekly for files, daily for database.

- Select a remote storage location to save backups (e.g., Google Drive, Dropbox, Amazon S3). This protects backups from server failures.

Step 3: Perform Your First Backup

- Go to the Current **Status** tab.
- Click **Backup Now** to create an immediate backup.

Restoring Your Site from a Backup

In case of an emergency, you can restore your website to a previous state easily:

- Open UpdraftPlus dashboard.
- Under **Existing Backups**, find the backup you want to restore.
- Click **Restore** and select which components (plugins, themes, uploads, database) to restore.
- Follow on-screen prompts until restoration completes.

Best Practices for Backups

- **Store Backups Off-Site:** Never keep backups only on your hosting server. Use remote storage or download copies locally.

- **Test Your Backups:** Occasionally restore backups on a staging site to ensure they work correctly.

- **Keep Multiple Backup Versions:** Retain backups for several weeks or months to allow recovery from various points in time.

- **Schedule Regular Backups:** Automate to avoid forgetting. Frequency depends on how often you update your site.

Security and backups are the cornerstone of a reliable WordPress site. While firewalls and anti-malware plugins protect and detect threats, backups provide you peace of mind that no matter what occurs, your site can be recovered.

For beginners, starting with a well-configured firewall plugin like Wordfence, a reliable anti-malware scanner such as MalCare, and an automated backup solution like UpdraftPlus addresses most dangers without overwhelming technical complexity.

Restoring Your Site from Backups: Step-by-Step Guide

Having a backup is only half the battle. When things go wrong—be it due to hacking, a plugin malfunction, or unintentional deletion—you need to restore your website promptly to minimize downtime and data loss. Understanding the restoration method permits you to recover your site without stress or pricey professional support.

Types of Backups You Might Have

Before diving into restoration steps, it's important to identify what kind of backups you have:

- **Full Site Backup:** Includes all WordPress files (themes, plugins, uploads) plus the database. This is the best type for complete restoration.

- **Database-Only Backup:** Contains only your site's database (content, settings, users). You'll still need WordPress files intact for a full restore.

- **File-Only Backup:** Just the WordPress files without database; useful if the content is intact but files are corrupted.

Knowing what you have helps tailor the restoration method.

Step-by-Step Restoration Using a Backup Plugin (UpdraftPlus Example)

If you have used a backup plugin like UpdraftPlus, the restore process is straightforward.

Step 1: Access Your WordPress Dashboard

- Log in to your WordPress admin panel.
- If your site is inaccessible, you may need to reinstall WordPress manually and then install the backup plugin before restoration.

Step 2: Go to Backup Plugin Settings

- From the dashboard, click **Settings** > **UpdraftPlus Backups** (or your chosen backup plugin)
- Click the **Existing Backups** tab to view stored backups.

Step 3: Choose a Backup to Restore

- Select the backup you want to restore based on date and completeness.
- Click **Restore**.

Step 4: Select Components to Restore

- Choose which parts of the backup to restore: plugins, themes, uploads, database, or others.
- For full restoration, select all.

Step 5: Start the Restoration Process

- Confirm and begin the restoration.
- The plugin will extract files and replace current site data with the backup version.
- This process may take several minutes depending on your site size.

Step 6: Test Your Site

- After restoration completes, visit your website frontend and backend to ensure everything works as expected.
- Clear your browser cache and WordPress caches if you use caching plugins.

Manual Restoration via FTP and phpMyAdmin

If a backup plugin is not available or your site is completely down, manual restoration is necessary.

Step 1: Upload WordPress Files via FTP

- Use an FTP client such as FileZilla to connect to your hosting server.

- Upload your backup WordPress files to the root directory (usually public_html). Overwrite existing files.

Step 2: Restore the Database

- Log into your hosting control panel and open **phpMyAdmin**.
- Select your WordPress database.
- Import your .sql backup file to overwrite the current database. This replaces your site content and settings.

Step 3: Update wp-config.php If Needed

- Ensure your wp-config.php file contains the correct database credentials if your hosting or database has changed.

Step 4: Check Site Functionality

- Test your website thoroughly for broken links, missing images, or errors.

Things to Keep in Mind When Restoring

- Restoring a backup will overwrite recent changes made after the backup date. Plan restoration during low-traffic times.

- Keep multiple backup copies in case one is corrupted.

- After restoring, update WordPress, themes, and plugins immediately to patch vulnerabilities.

Managing User Access and Monitoring Site Activity

Every user with access to your WordPress site is a possible security risk. Unauthorized or negligent users can unwittingly cause damage or open security weaknesses. Managing who has access and what permissions they hold is critical for maintaining security.

Understanding WordPress User Roles

WordPress comes with several built-in user roles, each with different capabilities:

- **Administrator:** Full control over the site, including installing plugins, editing themes, and managing users.
- **Editor:** Can publish and manage posts and pages, including those of others.
- **Author:** Can publish and manage their own posts.
- **Contributor:** Can write and manage their own posts but cannot publish them.

- **Subscriber:** Can only manage their profile.

Only assign administrator roles to trusted individuals to reduce risk.

Best Practices for Managing User Access

1. **Limit Administrator Accounts:** Keep the number of administrators to a minimum.
2. **Use Strong Passwords and 2FA:** For all users, especially those with elevated privileges.
3. **Review User Accounts Regularly:** Remove inactive users or those no longer involved.
4. **Assign Appropriate Roles:** Give users only the capabilities they need to perform their tasks.

Monitoring Site Activity

Keeping track of who does what on your site helps detect suspicious behavior early.

How to Monitor User Activity on WordPress

1. **Enable Activity Logs:** Use plugins such as *WP Activity Log* or *Activity Log* to record user actions.

2. **Review Login Attempts:** Security plugins like Wordfence track login attempts and notify you of failures or unusual patterns.

3. **Set Up Email Alerts:** Get notified immediately of new user registrations, password changes, or plugin installations.

4. **Monitor File Changes:** Some plugins scan for unexpected file modifications that may indicate a breach.

Responding to Suspicious Activity

If you notice unusual actions such as unknown users, repeated failed logins, or changes you didn't authorize:

- Temporarily disable affected user accounts.
- Change all administrator passwords immediately.
- Perform a full malware scan on your site.
- Restore from a backup if you suspect a breach.

What to Do If Your Site Gets Hacked: Immediate Action Plan

Recognizing Signs Your Site Has Been Hacked

Hacking signs vary but may include:

- Your site is down or inaccessible.
- Unexpected changes to content or appearance.
- Redirects to unknown or suspicious websites.
- Warnings from browsers or Google about malware.
- Unknown user accounts or administrative changes.
- Increased spam or phishing emails from your domain.

Step 1: Stay Calm and Assess the Situation

Panic can lead to mistakes. Take a deep breath and carefully review what is happening.

Step 2: Put Your Site into Maintenance Mode

Temporarily disable public access to prevent further damage or harm to visitors. Use a maintenance plugin or ask your hosting provider for assistance.

Step 3: Change Passwords Immediately

Reset passwords for all administrator and user accounts, including FTP, hosting control panel, and database access.

Step 4: Inform Your Hosting Provider

Many hosts offer support for hacked sites, including scanning and cleaning assistance. They can also temporarily suspend the site if needed.

Step 5: Run a Security Scan

Use your anti-malware plugin or external tools like *Sucuri SiteCheck* to identify infected files or suspicious code.

Step 6: Restore From a Clean Backup

If you have a backup taken before the hack, restore your site fully. Ensure the backup is clean and free from malware.

Step 7: Remove Suspicious Files Manually

If no clean backup is available, use FTP or hosting file manager to manually remove unknown files or code. This requires technical skill; consider professional help if unsure.

Step 8: Update Everything

Update WordPress core, themes, plugins, and passwords to close vulnerabilities exploited by hackers.

Step 9: Harden Your Security

After cleanup, strengthen your security by enabling firewalls, two-factor authentication, and restricting file permissions.

Step 10: Monitor Closely

Keep an eye on logs and site behavior for any signs of reinfection or lingering issues.

Step 11: Inform Your Users If Necessary

If your site handles user data, notify users about the breach and recommend password changes for their accounts.

Preventing Future Hacks

- Regularly update WordPress and plugins.
- Use security plugins with firewalls and malware scanning.
- Limit user access and monitor site activity.
- Backup your site frequently and test restorations.
- Educate yourself and team members about security best practices.

Security and backups are the backbone of a stable WordPress site. Understanding how to restore your site quickly, restricting user access carefully, and having a clear plan if your site is hacked will save you time, money, and stress.

By following the instructions in this chapter, even beginners may maintain a secure site that protects their information and visitors in 2025 and beyond.

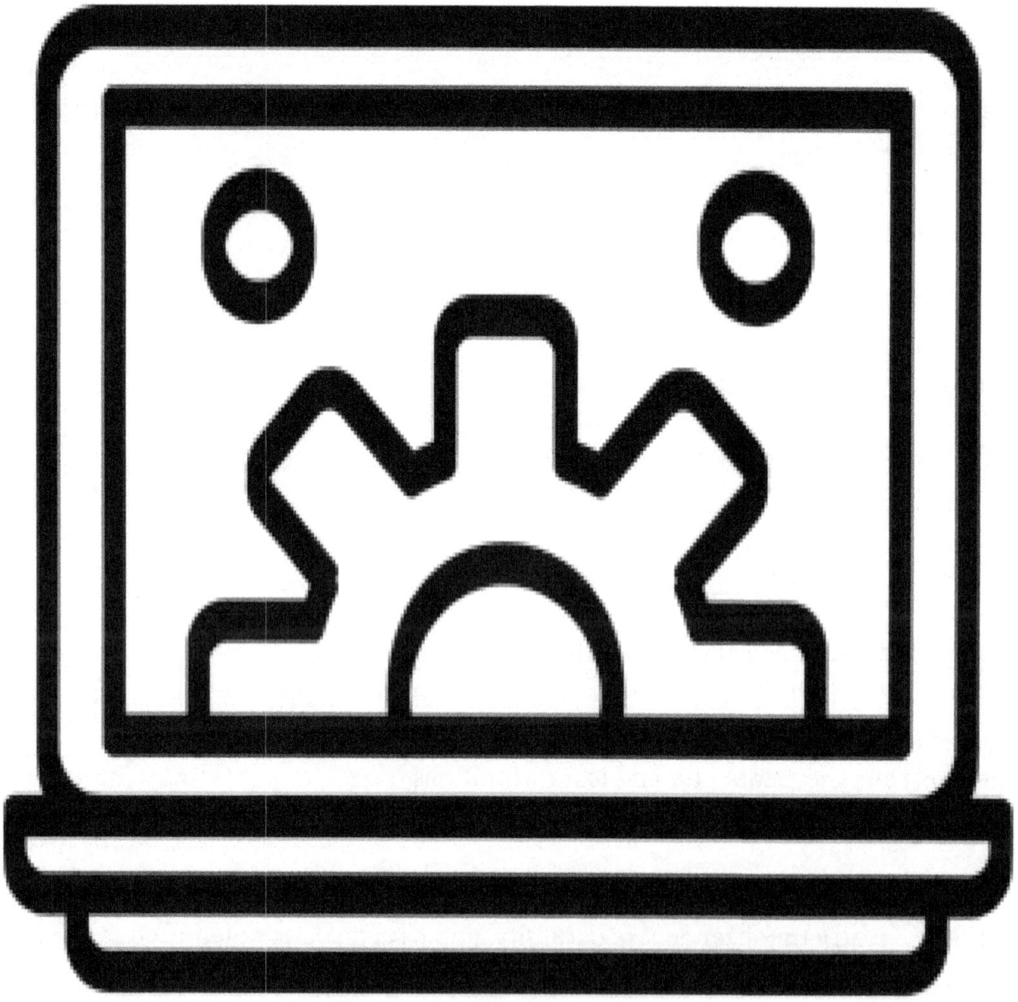

Chapter 10

SEO and Analytics for WordPress Beginners

Did you realize that nearly 90% of internet experiences begin with a search engine? Whether your website is a personal blog, an online store, or a company landing page, ranking prominently in search results is vital to attracting people. Search Engine Optimization (SEO) is the method that makes your website visible and attractive to search engines like Google, Bing, and Yahoo.

In 2025, SEO remains one of the most potent strategies to boost organic traffic without relying entirely on paid advertising. With millions of websites competing for attention, having a well-optimized WordPress site can set you out from the crowd.

What Is SEO?

SEO comprises optimizing your website's content, structure, and technological features to rank higher in search engine results pages (SERPs). Higher ranks mean more clicks, which translates into higher traffic, leads, and income.

Search engines utilize complex algorithms to pick which sites to show for every given query. These algorithms analyze hundreds of parameters, including relevancy, authority, user experience, and site performance.

Why SEO Matters for WordPress Beginners

1. **Attracts Targeted Traffic:** SEO helps your ideal audience find you organically when searching for topics or products you offer.

2. **Builds Credibility and Trust:** Sites ranking higher are seen as more trustworthy by users.

3. **Offers Long-Term Results:** Unlike paid ads, good SEO work can continue bringing visitors for months or years.

4. **Improves User Experience:** Many SEO practices enhance site speed, mobile usability, and content quality.

5. **Increases Conversion Opportunities:** More relevant visitors mean better chances to achieve your site's goals.

Key SEO Concepts to Understand

Before diving into plugins and settings, here are some foundational SEO terms you should know:

- **Keywords:** Words or phrases people type into search engines. Selecting the right keywords helps you target relevant traffic.

- **On-Page SEO:** Optimizations made directly on your website, such as content quality, meta tags, and URL structure.

- **Off-Page SEO:** Actions taken outside your website to improve authority, like backlinks from other sites.

- **Technical SEO:** Website backend optimizations, including site speed, mobile-friendliness, and XML sitemaps.

- **Meta Title and Description:** Snippets displayed in search results; they influence click-through rates.

- **Sitemap:** A file listing all your site's pages to help search engines index your content efficiently.

Installing and Configuring SEO Plugins

Optimizing SEO manually can be hard and time-consuming, especially for novices. Luckily, WordPress offers powerful SEO plugins that simplify this procedure. Two of the most popular and beginner-friendly plugins are Yoast SEO and Rank Math.

Why Use SEO Plugins?

SEO plugins help by:

- Guiding content optimization with real-time analysis and suggestions.
- Automatically generating XML sitemaps to improve indexing.

- Managing meta titles and descriptions without coding.
- Controlling which pages are indexed or excluded.
- Integrating social media metadata for better sharing.
- Monitoring site health and SEO performance.

Installing Yoast SEO

Step 1: Install and Activate Yoast SEO

- From your WordPress dashboard, go to **Plugins > Add New**.
- Search for "Yoast SEO."
- Click **Install Now** and then **Activate**.

Step 2: Run the Configuration Wizard

- Upon activation, a notification will prompt you to configure the plugin.
- Click **Configure Yoast SEO** to open the setup wizard.
- The wizard guides you through essential settings, including:
  - Site type (blog, online store, portfolio, etc.)
  - Organization or person info
  - Visibility preferences for post types
  - Connecting to webmaster tools
  - Title settings

Step 3: Set Up XML Sitemaps

- Yoast SEO automatically generates XML sitemaps.
- You can view your sitemap by appending /sitemap_index.xml to your site URL (e.g., yoursite.com/sitemap_index.xml).
- Submit this sitemap URL to Google Search Console to help Google discover your pages faster.

Step 4: Optimize Meta Titles and Descriptions

- On each post or page edit screen, scroll to the Yoast SEO box.
- Enter a keyword or key phrase to focus on.
- Edit the SEO title and meta description snippets, guided by Yoast's color-coded analysis
- Aim for green indicators to improve SEO readability and relevance.

Installing Rank Math SEO

Rank Math is a newer plugin gaining popularity for its feature-rich free version and beginner-friendly design.

Step 1: Install and Activate Rank Math

- Go to **Plugins** > **Add New** in your WordPress dashboard.
- Search for "Rank Math."
- Click **Install Now** and then **Activate**.

Step 2: Use the Setup Wizard

- After activation, Rank Math launches a setup wizard.
- You'll be asked to connect a free Rank Math account (optional but recommended for access to updates).
- Configure site type, webmaster tools integration, and SEO settings.
- Import settings if you previously used Yoast SEO.

Step 3: Configure Sitemaps

- Rank Math creates XML sitemaps by default.
- You can customize sitemap settings under **Rank Math** > **Sitemap Settings**.

Step 4: Optimize Content Using Rank Math Meta Box

- On editing posts and pages, the Rank Math box appears below the content editor.
- Enter your focus keyword to get real-time SEO analysis.
- Follow suggestions on keyword density, readability, internal linking, and meta tags.

Comparing Yoast SEO and Rank Math

Feature	Yoast SEO	Rank Math
User Interface	Intuitive, widely used	Modern, feature-rich
Keyword Optimization	Focus on one keyword (Pro version for multiple)	Multiple keywords (free)
XML Sitemap	Automatic, minimal configuration	Customizable with more options

Schema Markup	Basic schema support	Advanced schema support
Google Search Console	Integration available	Integrated and detailed
Price	Free + Premium version	Free + Paid options

Both plugins are excellent choices for beginners. Your decision depends on your specific needs and preferences.

Essential SEO Settings After Plugin Installation

Regardless of your chosen plugin, here are SEO settings to prioritize:

- **Permalink Structure:** Set URLs to be clean and descriptive. Recommended: /post-name/. Configure this under **Settings > Permalinks**.

- **Search Engine Visibility:** Ensure your site is visible to search engines by unchecking any "Discourage search engines from indexing this site" option.

- **Meta Robots Settings:** Control indexing of specific pages or post types to avoid duplicate content.

- **Breadcrumbs:** Enable breadcrumbs for better user experience and improved search appearance.

- **Social Integration:** Add Open Graph and Twitter Card metadata so your content looks appealing when shared.

Crafting SEO-Friendly Content

SEO plugins provide tools, but content quality remains king. Keep these tips in mind:

- Research keywords relevant to your audience.
- Write clear, engaging, and original content.
- Use headings and bullet points for easy reading.
- Optimize images with descriptive alt text.
- Link internally to related content.
- Keep meta descriptions concise and compelling.

Monitoring Your SEO Performance

Install Google Search Console and Google Analytics to track your site's search performance and visitor activity. Both tools provide invaluable insights on keywords, rankings, site issues, and traffic sources.

SEO is a fundamental skill for any WordPress site owner. Using plugins like Yoast SEO or Rank Math simplifies the hard work of optimizing your site for search engines, helping you reach more users.

Optimizing Titles for Maximum Impact

What Is a Title Tag?

A title tag is an HTML element that specifies the title of a webpage. It appears as the clickable headline on search engine results pages (SERPs) and at the top of a browser window or tab.

Best Practices for Title Tags

1. **Keep It Concise and Clear:** Search engines generally display up to 60 characters of the title. Aim to convey the main topic within this limit to avoid truncation.

2. **Include Target Keywords:** Incorporate your primary keyword naturally near the beginning of the title to signal relevance.

3. **Be Unique for Each Page:** Each page or post should have a distinct title to avoid confusion and duplication.

4. **Use Action Words or Numbers:** Titles with action verbs or numbers (e.g., "7 Tips to…" or "How to…") tend to attract more clicks.

5. **Match User Intent:** Make sure the title aligns with what users are searching for to increase relevance and CTR.

How to Edit Titles in WordPress

SEO plugins like Yoast SEO and Rank Math make this easy:

- When editing a post or page, scroll to the SEO plugin's meta box.
- Find the **SEO Title** field and enter your optimized title.

- Preview how it will appear on Google using the snippet preview tool.

Crafting Effective Meta Descriptions

What Is a Meta Description?

The meta description is a brief summary of a webpage's content shown beneath the title in search results. While it doesn't directly impact rankings, it strongly influences whether users decide to click.

Best Practices for Meta Descriptions

1. **Length:** Keep descriptions between 150-160 characters to prevent truncation.

2. **Clear and Compelling:** Write in a way that entices users to visit your site by highlighting benefits or solving a problem.

3. **Use Keywords Thoughtfully:** Include primary keywords naturally, as search engines highlight these words in bold, catching users' attention.

4. **Avoid Duplication:** Ensure every page has a unique meta description to avoid confusion.

5. **Call to Action:** Adding phrases like "Learn how," "Discover," or "Get started" encourages clicks.

Editing Meta Descriptions in WordPress

Using SEO plugins, the process is similar to titles:

- Open the post or page editor.
- Scroll to the SEO meta box.
- Locate the **Meta Description** field and type your description.
- Use the preview to see how it looks in search results.

Structuring Clean and SEO-Friendly URLs

Why URLs Matter

URLs are the addresses users see and share. Clean URLs improve user experience, help search engines understand content structure, and can enhance your SEO.

Characteristics of SEO-Friendly URLs

1. **Readable and Simple:** URLs should be easy to read and remember, avoiding random numbers or symbols.

2. **Use Keywords:** Include relevant keywords that describe the page content clearly.

3. **Use Hyphens to Separate Words:** Hyphens improve readability and are preferred by search engines over underscores or spaces.

4. **Avoid Stop Words:** Words like "and," "or," "the," can often be omitted for brevity.

5. **Keep URLs Short:** Shorter URLs are easier to share and less likely to be truncated.

Configuring URLs in WordPress

- Go to **Settings** > **Permalinks** in your dashboard.
- Select the **Post name** option to use SEO-friendly URLs (e.g., yoursite.com/sample-post).
- Save changes.

When creating posts or pages, WordPress automatically generates the URL slug based on the title. You can edit this slug for clarity and SEO by clicking the **Edit** button next to the permalink in the editor.

Using Sitemaps Effectively

What Is a Sitemap?

A sitemap is a file that lists all important pages on your website, helping search engines crawl and index your site efficiently.

153

Types of Sitemaps

- **XML Sitemap:** Designed for search engines, listing URLs and metadata like last update date and priority.

- **HTML Sitemap:** Designed for visitors to find content easily, often linked from the footer or sidebar.

Benefits of Using XML Sitemaps

- Faster and more comprehensive indexing by search engines.
- Easier discovery of new or updated pages.
- Can highlight priority pages and update frequencies.

How to Generate Sitemaps in WordPress

Most SEO plugins generate sitemaps automatically:

- **Yoast SEO:** Enabled by default. Access it via yoursite.com/sitemap_index.xml.

- **Rank Math:** Also automatically creates sitemaps; settings available under **Rank Math > Sitemap Settings**.

Submitting Your Sitemap to Search Engines

1. Sign up or log in to **Google Search Console** and **Bing Webmaster Tools**.
2. Add your website property.
3. Submit your sitemap URL (e.g., yoursite.com/sitemap_index.xml).
4. Monitor indexing status and fix errors reported.

Robots.txt: Controlling Search Engine Crawling

What Is Robots.txt?

robots.txt is a text file placed in your website's root directory that instructs search engine bots which pages or sections they can or cannot crawl.

Why Use Robots.txt?

- Prevent indexing of duplicate or private content.
- Save crawl budget for important pages.

- Block sensitive files or admin areas from being indexed.

Basic Structure of Robots.txt

txt
Copy
User-agent: *
Disallow: /wp-admin/
Disallow: /wp-login.php
Allow: /wp-admin/admin-ajax.php

This example tells all bots not to crawl the admin area, but allows AJAX requests.

Managing Robots.txt in WordPress

- Some SEO plugins (Yoast SEO, Rank Math) allow editing robots.txt directly from the dashboard.

- Alternatively, use FTP or hosting file manager to create or edit the robots.txt file in your root directory.

Best Practices for Robots.txt

- Do not block your sitemap URL.
- Avoid blocking CSS or JavaScript files needed to render pages properly.
- Use caution when disallowing URLs to prevent accidentally hiding important content.

Putting It All Together: How These Elements Work in Harmony

Optimized titles, meta descriptions, and URLs make your sites beautiful and understandable for users and search engines. Sitemaps help search engines identify and index your material fast. Robots.txt directs bots to avoid irrelevant or sensitive regions, focusing crawl power on useful pages.

Together, these aspects provide a robust SEO foundation that boosts results, generates traffic, and enhances user experience.

Mastering these SEO foundations empowers you to manage how your WordPress site appears and performs in search results. By carefully writing titles, meta descriptions, and URLs, and managing sitemaps and robots.txt files, you develop a site that both people and search engines adore.

Setting Up Website Analytics for Your WordPress Site

To analyze your website traffic, you need a reliable analytics tool. The industry standard is **Google Analytics**, a free service that provides detailed reports about your visitors.

Installing Google Analytics on WordPress

1. **Create a Google Analytics Account:**
   Visit analytics.google.com, sign in with your Google account, and create a new property for your website.

2. **Get the Tracking ID:**
   Google Analytics will provide you with a unique tracking code or ID.

3. **Connect Google Analytics to WordPress:**

   - Use a plugin like *MonsterInsights* or *Site Kit by Google*.
   - Install and activate your chosen plugin from the WordPress dashboard.
   - Follow the plugin's setup wizard to authenticate and link your Google Analytics account.

Once set up, Google Analytics begins collecting data immediately, but it takes some time to accumulate meaningful insights.

Key Metrics to Track and What They Mean

1. Users and Sessions

- *Users* represent unique visitors to your site.
- *Sessions* are the total number of visits, including repeat visits by the same user.

Monitoring users and sessions helps you understand the size and engagement level of your audience.

2. Pageviews

The total number of pages viewed. More pageviews indicate users explore your site, but consider this alongside session duration.

3. Average Session Duration

Shows how long visitors stay on your site. Longer durations usually mean better engagement.

4. Bounce Rate

The percentage of visitors who leave after viewing only one page. A high bounce rate might signal content or usability issues.

5. Traffic Sources

Reveals where visitors come from—search engines, social media, direct visits, or referrals. Understanding sources helps allocate your marketing efforts effectively.

6. Behavior Flow

Visualizes the path visitors take through your site, showing popular pages and where users drop off.

Interpreting Traffic Data to Improve Your Site

Data without context is just numbers. Use these insights to make targeted improvements:

- **Identify High-Performing Content:** Pages with high traffic and long session durations are valuable. Analyze what works—topics, format, keywords—and replicate this success.

- **Fix Pages with High Bounce Rates:** Low engagement pages may need better content, faster loading, or clearer calls to action.

- **Focus on Top Traffic Sources:** Invest in channels bringing the most visitors, or explore why others underperform.

- **Track Mobile vs. Desktop Users:** Optimize your site's design and speed for the dominant devices your audience uses.

Advanced Analytics Tools for WordPress

While Google Analytics is powerful, additional tools can deepen your understanding:

- **Google Search Console:** Tracks search performance, indexing status, and site errors.
- **Hotjar:** Visualizes user behavior through heatmaps and session recordings.
- **Ahrefs or SEMrush:** Provides competitive analysis and keyword tracking.

Tips to Improve Your Rankings in 2025's Search Landscape

SEO continues to evolve. To succeed in 2025, follow these strategies:

1. Prioritize User Experience (UX)

Google rewards sites that provide seamless experiences. Ensure your site is fast, mobile-friendly, and easy to navigate.

2. Focus on Intent-Driven Content

Create content that matches what users truly want—informational, transactional, or navigational.

3. Optimize for Voice Search

With the rise of digital assistants, use natural language and long-tail keywords.

4. Use Structured Data

Implement schema markup to enhance search listings with rich snippets.

5. Build Quality Backlinks

Earn links from reputable sites to boost your authority.

6. Regularly Update Content

Keep your information current to maintain relevance and rankings.

Tracking and interpreting website traffic data offers you the knowledge to optimize your site and develop your audience. Combined with effective SEO methods adapted for 2025's landscape, your WordPress site can thrive in search results and beyond.

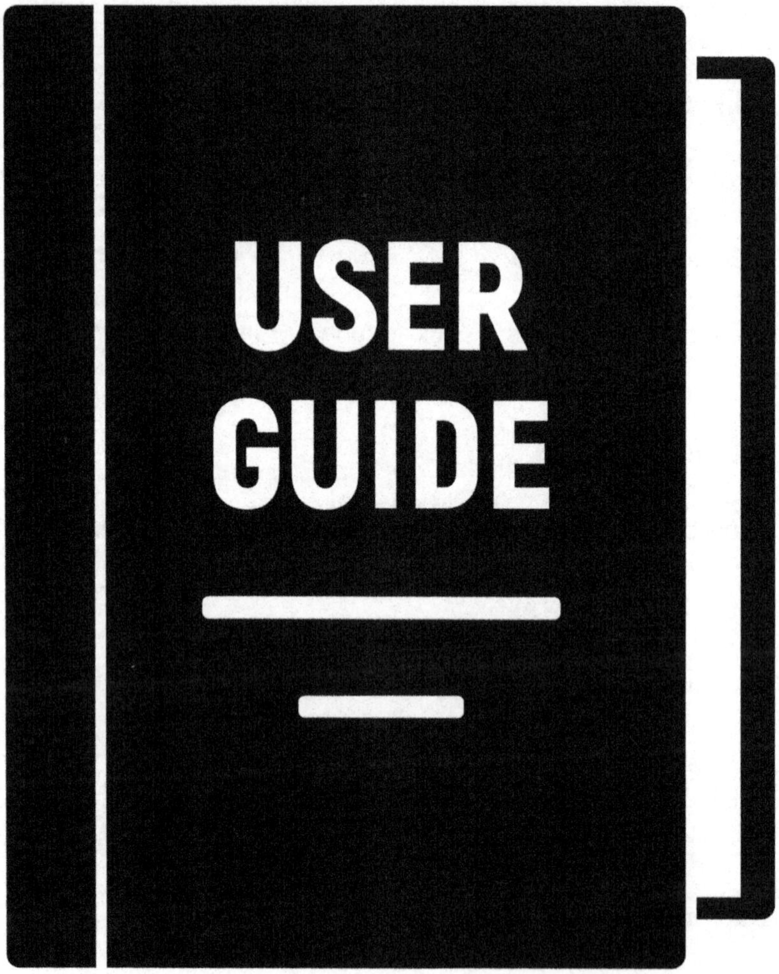
USER
GUIDE

Chapter 11

Monetizing Your WordPress Website

Did you know that as of 2025, over 60% of small businesses globally use websites as a key source of revenue generation? Whether you're running a blog, portfolio, or company website, WordPress offers strong tools to transform your online presence into a source of cash. Monetizing your website is no longer a hard problem reserved for experts. With the appropriate tactics and plugins, even beginners can establish sustainable money streams.

In this chapter, you will study several monetization methods—from showing advertisements and affiliate marketing to selling products and services—and learn how to build up a fully functional online store using WooCommerce, the world's leading WordPress e-commerce plugin.

Overview of Monetization Options for WordPress

Your website can produce cash through many avenues. Choosing the right blend relies on your audience, content, and business model. Let's analyze the primary monetization strategies available for WordPress sites.

1. Displaying Advertisements

One of the most common ways to earn money from your website is through advertisements. Ads can be in the form of banners, videos, or native ads strategically placed within your content.

- **Google AdSense:** The most popular ad network, AdSense automatically displays relevant ads and pays you based on clicks or impressions.

- **Other Ad Networks:** Alternatives include Media.net, AdThrive, or Ezoic, each with specific requirements and revenue models.

- **Direct Advertising:** You can sell ad space directly to businesses related to your niche, often at higher rates.

Benefits:

- Easy to implement, especially with WordPress ad management plugins.
- Passive income once set up.

Considerations:

- Revenue depends heavily on traffic volume.
- Too many ads can affect user experience negatively.

---

2. Affiliate Marketing

Affiliate marketing involves promoting other companies' products or services on your site and earning a commission for each sale or lead generated through your referral links.

- **Popular Affiliate Programs:** Amazon Associates, ShareASale, Commission Junction, and many niche-specific programs.

- **Integration:** WordPress plugins like ThirstyAffiliates help manage and cloak affiliate links.

- **Content Ideas:** Product reviews, tutorials, or curated lists are effective for affiliate marketing.

Benefits:

- No inventory or customer service required.
- Scalable with quality content.

Considerations:

- Requires trust and transparency with your audience.
- Compliance with affiliate program rules and disclosure laws is mandatory.

---

3. Selling Products

You can sell physical or digital products directly from your WordPress site. This approach gives you control over pricing, branding, and customer relationships.

- **Physical Products:** Tangible items such as crafts, merchandise, or books.
- **Digital Products:** Ebooks, courses, software, music, or art downloads.

Benefits:

- Potential for high-profit margins, especially with digital products.

- Builds brand authority and customer loyalty.

Considerations:

- Requires inventory management for physical goods.
- Digital products need secure delivery mechanisms.

---

4. Offering Services

Many WordPress websites are built around offering services such as consulting, coaching, design, writing, or freelance work.

- **Booking and Scheduling:** Plugins like Bookly or Amelia enable clients to schedule appointments online.

- **Payment Integration:** Accept payments securely through PayPal, Stripe, or other gateways.

- **Showcasing Portfolio:** Use WordPress themes and plugins designed for service providers to highlight expertise.

Benefits:

- Monetize your skills directly.
- Often less competition compared to product sales.

Considerations:

- Time-intensive and may require client management systems.
- Building credibility is crucial.

Setting Up an Online Store with WooCommerce

For those interested in selling products or services online, WooCommerce is the premier ecommerce plugin for WordPress. It transforms your site into a powerful online store with extensive customization options.

Why Choose WooCommerce?

- **Free Core Plugin:** Most essential features are available at no cost.
- **Flexibility:** Sell physical and digital products, manage inventory, and configure shipping and tax options.
- **Extensive Add-Ons:** Thousands of plugins and themes integrate seamlessly with WooCommerce.
- **Large Community:** Active support and constant updates ensure reliability.

Step-by-Step Guide to Installing WooCommerce

Step 1: Install the WooCommerce Plugin

- Log in to your WordPress dashboard.
- Go to **Plugins > Add New**.
- Search for "WooCommerce."
- Click **Install Now** and then **Activate**.

Step 2: Run the Setup Wizard

Upon activation, WooCommerce launches a setup wizard to configure your store:

- **Store Details:** Enter your location, currency, and the types of products you plan to sell.
- **Payment Methods:** Choose payment gateways like PayPal, Stripe, or offline payments.
- **Shipping Options:** Define shipping zones, rates, and delivery methods.
- **Recommended Plugins:** WooCommerce suggests extensions like automated tax calculators or enhanced payment gateways.

Adding Your First Products

Step 1: Add New Product

- Go to **Products > Add New**.
- Enter the product name and detailed description.

Step 2: Set Product Data

- Choose the product type: simple, grouped, virtual, downloadable, or variable.
- Set price, SKU (stock-keeping unit), inventory status, and shipping details.

- Upload product images and galleries to showcase your items.

Step 3: Publish

- Review your product details.
- Click **Publish** to make the product live in your store.

Customizing Your Storefront

- Use WooCommerce-compatible themes designed for online stores for a professional appearance.
- Add widgets for product categories, filters, and shopping carts.
- Set up promotional banners and featured products on your homepage.

Managing Orders and Customers

- WooCommerce provides an intuitive dashboard to track orders, update statuses, and communicate with customers.
- Set up email notifications for new orders, shipping updates, and customer inquiries.
- Use reports to monitor sales, stock levels, and customer data.

Extending WooCommerce Functionality

- **Subscriptions:** Offer recurring payments for memberships or products.
- **Bookings:** Sell appointments or rentals with scheduling features.
- **Reviews and Ratings:** Encourage customer feedback to build trust.
- **Marketing Tools:** Integrate with email marketing platforms and social media.

Tips for Successful Monetization

- Focus on quality content and user experience to attract and retain visitors.
- Use multiple monetization strategies to diversify income sources.
- Understand your audience's needs and tailor products or services accordingly.
- Regularly analyze sales data and adjust your offerings and marketing.
- Comply with legal requirements such as privacy policies, tax regulations, and refund policies.

Monetizing your WordPress blog is doable with the appropriate approach and tools. Whether through advertising, affiliate marketing, product sales, or services, WordPress allows the freedom to establish revenue sources that meet your aims. WooCommerce, in particular, permits newcomers to set up fully working online storefronts with ease.

Unlocking Recurring Revenue: Using Membership and Subscription Plugins

In today's digital economy, recurring revenue models have altered how websites generate cash. By delivering unique material, products, or services behind a membership or subscription, website owners can assure stable, predictable cash streams. Research reveals that organizations employing subscription models grow revenue 5 times faster than those relying purely on one-time transactions.

WordPress gives great capabilities to develop such membership experiences, helping you reward loyal users while building long-term relationships.

What Are Membership and Subscription Plugins?

These plugins enable you to restrict access to certain areas of your website — like articles, videos, forums, or downloadable stuff — to paying members. You can create several membership levels with varying access capabilities and periodic billing choices.

Benefits of Using Membership and Subscription Plugins

- **Stable Income:** Subscriptions provide predictable monthly or annual revenue.
- **Community Building:** Foster engagement with exclusive content and member forums.
- **Flexible Access Control:** Limit content or products based on membership tiers.
- **Integrated Payments:** Handle recurring billing, upgrades, and cancellations seamlessly.
- **Content Dripping:** Schedule content delivery over time to keep members engaged.

Popular Membership and Subscription Plugins for WordPress

- **MemberPress:** A comprehensive plugin with easy setup, powerful access rules, and robust payment integrations.

- **Restrict Content Pro:** Lightweight and developer-friendly, great for content access control.

- **Paid Memberships Pro:** Offers a free core plugin with premium add-ons for extended features.

- **WooCommerce Memberships:** Integrates tightly with WooCommerce for combined product and membership sales.

Setting Up a Membership Site with MemberPress (Example)

Step 1: Install and Activate MemberPress

- Purchase MemberPress from its official website.
- Upload the plugin via your WordPress dashboard under **Plugins > Add New > Upload Plugin**.
- Activate and enter your license key.

Step 2: Configure Membership Levels

- Go to **MemberPress > Memberships > Add New**.
- Create a membership level name (e.g., Basic, Premium).
- Set pricing, billing frequency, and trial period if any.

Step 3: Set Access Rules

- Define which pages, posts, categories, or files are accessible to each membership level.
- Go to **MemberPress > Rules > Add New** to set these restrictions.

Step 4: Configure Payment Gateways

- Under **MemberPress > Options > Payments**, set up payment processors like PayPal, Stripe, or Authorize.net.

Step 5: Design Membership Pages

- Customize sign-up, login, and account pages to match your brand.

Creating a Compelling Membership Offer

- Provide unique, high-value content members can't find elsewhere.
- Offer perks like early access, discounts, or exclusive community forums.
- Use content dripping to release material gradually, maintaining engagement.

Creating and Selling Online Courses or Digital Downloads

The e-learning market is booming, expected to surpass $400 billion globally by 2026. Online courses and digital products like ebooks, templates, and software offer high-profit margins and scalable income without inventory concerns.

WordPress Plugins for Course Creation and Digital Sales

- **LearnDash:** A top-rated LMS (Learning Management System) plugin offering course builder, quizzes, certificates, and integrations.

- **LifterLMS:** Powerful and user-friendly LMS with membership and subscription options.

- **Easy Digital Downloads (EDD):** Specializes in selling digital products with built-in payment processing.

- **WooCommerce:** Also supports digital product sales with extensive add-ons.

How to Create and Sell an Online Course with LearnDash

Step 1: Install and Activate LearnDash

- Purchase LearnDash from their website.
- Upload and activate the plugin in WordPress.

Step 2: Create Courses

- Go to **LearnDash LMS > Courses > Add New**.
- Add a course title and description.
- Use the built-in course builder to add lessons and topics.

Step 3: Set Up Quizzes and Certificates

- Enhance learning with quizzes and award completion certificates.

Step 4: Configure Pricing and Access

- Set course pricing or bundle multiple courses.
- Use memberships or subscription options to control access.

Step 5: Integrate Payment Gateways

- Connect to PayPal, Stripe, or other processors.

Selling Digital Downloads with Easy Digital Downloads (EDD)

Step 1: Install and Activate EDD

- From **Plugins > Add New**, search "Easy Digital Downloads."
- Install and activate.

Step 2: Add Your Digital Products

- Go to **Downloads > Add New**.
- Enter product title, description, and upload files.
- Set pricing and download limits if needed.

Step 3: Set Up Payment Gateways

- Configure payment options under **Downloads > Settings > Payment Gateways**.

Step 4: Customize Storefront

- Choose or customize themes to highlight your products professionally.

Tips for Successful Online Courses and Digital Products

- Research your audience's needs and pain points before creating products.
- Deliver high-quality content in video, text, and interactive formats.
- Provide excellent customer support and engage with learners.
- Use email marketing and social media to promote your offerings.
- Regularly update courses and products to maintain relevance.

Membership and subscription models, coupled online courses and digital downloads, offer scalable and attractive monetization possibilities for WordPress users in 2025. With the correct tools and technique, beginners can develop viable internet companies that generate recurring revenue and foster loyal communities.

Integrating Payment Gateways Securely

What Are Payment Gateways?

Payment gateways are services that process online payments, connecting your website to banks and credit card networks. They encrypt sensitive data, authorize transactions, and transmit payments securely.

Choosing the right payment gateway and integrating it properly is vital for client trust and smooth operations.

Popular Payment Gateways for WordPress

- **PayPal:** Widely recognized and trusted; supports one-time and recurring payments.
- **Stripe:** Highly customizable, supports credit cards, Apple Pay, and Google Pay.
- **Authorize.Net:** Longstanding, robust payment processor with advanced fraud tools.
- **Square:** Great for physical and online sales, integrates with POS systems.

Securing Your Payment Gateway Integration

Step 1: Use SSL Certificates: SSL encrypts data between your visitors and your site. Ensure your website has a valid SSL certificate, indicated by "https://" and a padlock icon in browsers. Many hosting providers offer free SSL certificates via Let's Encrypt.

Step 2: Choose Reliable Plugins or Built-in Options: Use trusted WordPress plugins or WooCommerce extensions for payment gateways rather than custom coding. These are regularly updated to meet security standards.

Step 3: PCI Compliance: The Payment Card Industry Data Security Standard (PCI DSS) sets guidelines to protect cardholder data. Using gateways like Stripe or PayPal offloads PCI compliance responsibilities, as they handle payment data off-site.

Step 4: Keep Software Updated: Regularly update WordPress, plugins, and themes to patch vulnerabilities.

Step 5: Enable Fraud Detection Features: Many gateways provide tools like Address Verification System (AVS) and Card Verification Value (CVV) checks to reduce fraudulent transactions.

Step-by-Step Example: Setting Up Stripe in WooCommerce

1. **Install and Activate WooCommerce Stripe Payment Gateway Plugin**
2. **Go to WooCommerce > Settings > Payments**
3. **Enable Stripe and click Configure**
4. **Enter your Stripe API keys from your Stripe dashboard**
5. **Set payment options and save changes**
6. **Test payments using Stripe's test mode before going live**

Email Marketing and List Building with WordPress

Why Email Marketing Matters

Despite social media's popularity, email marketing remains the highest ROI digital marketing channel, with an average return of $42 for every dollar invested. Building and nurturing an email list helps you engage directly with your audience, promote items, and generate repeat sales.

Building an Email List on Your WordPress Site

Step 1: Choose an Email Marketing Service
Popular providers include Mailchimp, ConvertKit, AWeber, and ActiveCampaign. Many offer free tiers for beginners.

Step 2: Use WordPress Plugins to Connect Your Site

- *Mailchimp for WordPress*
- *ConvertKit for WordPress*
- *Newsletter*
- *Bloom*

These plugins help you create subscription forms, pop-ups, and manage contacts.

Step 3: Create Irresistible Opt-In Offers
Encourage visitors to subscribe by offering free downloads, discounts, or exclusive content.

Designing Effective Subscription Forms

- Keep forms simple, asking only for essential information (email and name).
- Place forms prominently: homepage, blog posts, footer, and exit intent pop-ups.
- Use clear calls to action like "Join Free" or "Get the Guide."

Automating Email Campaigns

Set up automated email sequences to welcome new subscribers, deliver content, or promote products. Email marketing services provide user-friendly builders to design these workflows without coding.

Complying with Email Laws

Include unsubscribe links and your physical business address in emails to comply with laws like CAN-SPAM and GDPR.

Legal Considerations: Privacy Policy, GDPR Compliance, and Terms of Service

Why Legal Compliance Is Non-Negotiable

With increased data breaches and privacy concerns, governments worldwide have enacted laws to protect consumers. Non-compliance can lead to heavy fines and loss of customer trust.

Privacy Policy

A privacy policy explains what data you collect, how you use it, and how you protect it. It must be accessible on your website, usually linked in the footer.

Key Elements to Include:

- Types of data collected (personal info, cookies, etc.)
- Purpose of data collection
- Data sharing with third parties
- User rights regarding their data
- How users can contact you about privacy concerns

GDPR Compliance

The General Data Protection Regulation (GDPR) applies if you collect data from residents of the European Union. It requires:

- Clear consent before collecting personal data.
- Ability for users to access, correct, or delete their data.
- Prompt notification of data breaches.
- Data Protection Officer appointment (for some businesses).

Use GDPR-compliant forms and cookie consent banners on your WordPress site.

Terms of Service

This document outlines rules and responsibilities between you and your users or customers, protecting your business legally.

Typical Sections:

- User conduct guidelines
- Payment terms
- Refund and cancellation policies
- Intellectual property rights
- Disclaimers and limitations of liability

Tools to Help Generate Legal Pages

- **Termly** and ** iubenda** offer generators for privacy policies and terms of service tailored for WordPress.
- Some SEO plugins include basic privacy policy templates.
- Always consult with a legal professional to customize your policies.

Successfully monetizing your WordPress website in 2025 includes more than drawing visitors—it demands safe payments, good communication with your audience, and legal compliance. Integrating payment gateways with security best practices protects your revenue and customers.

Building and nurturing an email list connects you directly with your audience, encouraging loyalty and increasing sales. Finally, precise legal policies secure your firm and generate confidence.

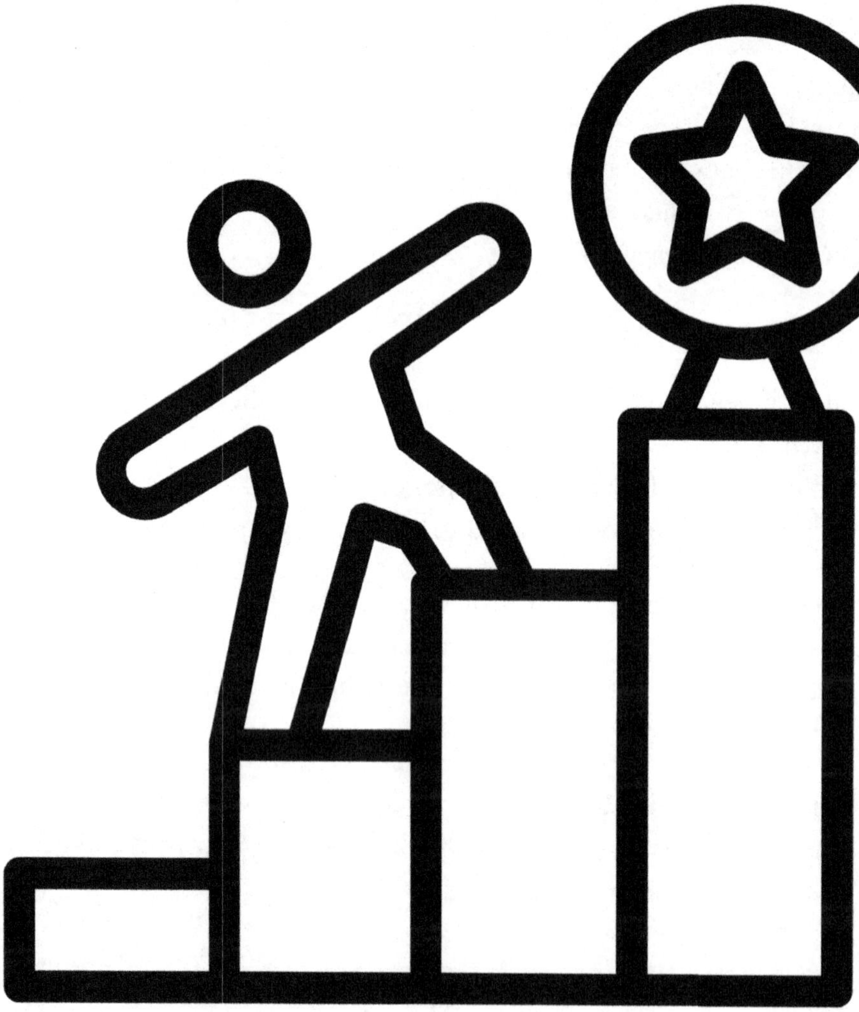

Chapter 12

Maintaining and Growing Your WordPress Site

Did you know that over 40% of website owners quit their sites owing to technical problems or lack of maintenance? WordPress drives roughly half the web, but even the strongest websites can crumble without regular attention. Maintaining your WordPress site isn't just about correcting problems—it's about establishing a pleasant, safe, and speedy experience for your visitors that fosters growth.

In 2025, with increasing cyber dangers and rising user demands, constant maintenance and safe experimentation are important. This chapter covers key continuing activities, cleanup procedures, performance tests, and the usage of staging environments to protect your live site while attempting new features or changes.

Regular Maintenance Tasks: Updates, Cleanup, and Performance Checks

Why Regular Maintenance Matters

A WordPress website is essentially a live ecosystem made up of the core software, themes, plugins, media, and content. Each part needs attention to perform effectively and securely. Neglect can lead to security breaches, poor load times, and broken functionality, which impact your reputation and search rankings.

Keeping WordPress Updated

Core WordPress Updates

WordPress regularly releases updates that fix bugs, improve security, and add new features. It's crucial to install these promptly:

- **Automatic Updates:** Since WordPress 5.5, automatic minor updates are enabled by default. You can enable or disable automatic major updates via filters if desired.

- **Manual Updates:** Navigate to the dashboard's **Updates** section and click **Update Now** when available.

Theme and Plugin Updates

Themes and plugins are developed by various authors and frequently receive updates.

- **Why Update?** Updates fix security vulnerabilities and add improvements.

- **How to Update Safely?** Backup your site before updating. Update one plugin at a time and test functionality after each.

- **Use Trusted Sources:** Only updates from official repositories or developers to avoid malicious code.

Cleaning Up Your WordPress Site

Over time, unused plugins, themes, and media files accumulate, increasing the site's size and possibly causing conflicts.

- **Remove Unused Plugins and Themes:** Deactivate and delete plugins and themes not in use.

- **Optimize Database:** Use plugins like *WP-Optimize* to clean post revisions, spam comments, and transient options.

- **Media Library Management:** Delete unused images or use tools like *Media Cleaner* to remove orphaned files.

- **Comment Moderation:** Regularly check and remove spam comments to reduce clutter and potential security risks.

Performance Checks and Optimization

Website speed directly affects user experience and SEO rankings. Regularly monitor and optimize performance.

Tools for Performance Monitoring

- **Google PageSpeed Insights:** Provides actionable tips and performance scores.
- **GTmetrix:** Offers detailed reports on load times and bottlenecks.
- **Pingdom:** Monitors uptime and site speed globally.

Common Performance Optimization Tasks

- **Caching:** Use caching plugins (e.g., *W3 Total Cache*, *WP Rocket*) to serve static pages faster.

- **Image Optimization:** Compress images without quality loss using plugins like *Smush* or *ShortPixel*.

- **Minify CSS and JavaScript:** Reduce file sizes to speed up loading.

- **Use a Content Delivery Network (CDN):** Distribute your site's static files globally to reduce latency.

- **Limit External Requests:** Reduce scripts and fonts loaded from third parties.

Using Staging Sites for Safe Testing and Updates

What Is a Staging Site?

A staging site is a clone of your live website hosted in a separate environment. It allows you to test updates, new plugins, themes, or custom code without risking your live site's functionality.

Why Use a Staging Site?

- **Prevent Downtime:** Test changes before applying them to your live site.
- **Avoid Broken Features:** Identify plugin conflicts or errors early.
- **Safe Customization:** Experiment with design or functionality without affecting visitors.
- **Client Approval:** Show changes to clients or stakeholders before going live.

Creating a Staging Site

Option 1: Using Hosting Provider Tools

Many managed WordPress hosts (e.g., Bluehost, SiteGround, WP Engine) offer one-click staging environments accessible via their control panels.

- Log into your hosting dashboard.
- Find the staging or clone feature.

- Create a staging copy of your site with a few clicks.

Option 2: Using Plugins

If your host doesn't provide staging, use plugins like:

- **WP Staging:** Creates a duplicate site in a subfolder or subdomain.
- **Duplicator:** Allows manual cloning and migration.

Testing on Your Staging Site

- Update plugins, themes, and WordPress core.
- Test new plugins or custom code.
- Verify forms, checkout processes, and interactive features.
- Check mobile responsiveness and browser compatibility.

Pushing Changes Live

Once you're confident updates work flawlessly:

- Use your host's staging tools to push changes to production.
- If using plugins, follow their specific steps for migration.
- Always backup your live site before applying updates.

Best Practices for Staging Environments

- Keep staging separate from search engines by requiring password access or noindex settings.

- Regularly refresh staging sites to mirror live content and plugins.

- Use staging for major changes, not daily content edits.

Maintaining your WordPress site is not only about preventing problems—it's about creating a platform that grows, adapts, and keeps producing value. Regular updates, maintenance, and performance optimization ensure your visitors have a quick, secure, and dependable experience. Using staging sites improves trust, enabling you to innovate without risk.

Handling Comments and Community Management

Why Comments Matter

Comments turn static content into dynamic interactions. They provide social proof, deepen interaction, and generate a dedicated audience. Visitors who remark feel valued and engaged, increasing the possibilities of return visits and shares.

Managing Comments in WordPress

WordPress includes built-in comment management tools. Here's how to make the most of them:

- **Moderation Settings:** Under **Settings > Discussion**, control when comments require approval before appearing.

- **Comment Notifications:** Enable email alerts for new comments to stay responsive.

- **Blacklist and Spam Filters:** Use the built-in spam filter and consider plugins like *Akismet* to block unwanted comments automatically.

Best Practices for Community Management

1. **Respond Promptly:** Engage with your commenters respectfully to foster dialogue.

2. **Set Clear Guidelines:** Publish a comment policy outlining acceptable behavior to keep discussions constructive.

3. **Encourage Positive Interaction:** Highlight thoughtful comments or featured community members.

4. **Handle Negative Comments Wisely:** Address criticism professionally; remove offensive or spam comments swiftly.

Enhancing Comments with Plugins

- **Disqus:** Provides advanced commenting features like threading, social login, and moderation tools.

- **wpDiscuz:** Offers real-time commenting and customizable forms.

- **Comment Likes and Subscriptions:** Encourage interaction by letting users like or subscribe to comment threads.

Leveraging Social Media Integration

Why Social Media Is Key to Growth

In 2025, over 4 billion people will use social media platforms globally. Connecting your WordPress site to social channels extends your reach, drives traffic, and builds your brand's voice.

Integrating Social Sharing Buttons

Make it easy for visitors to share your content using plugins such as:

- **Social Warfare:** Fast, customizable sharing buttons.
- **Monarch:** Elegant social sharing and follow buttons by Elegant Themes.
- **AddToAny:** Supports sharing across hundreds of platforms.

Place buttons strategically on posts, pages, and product pages to maximize visibility.

Displaying Social Feeds on Your Site

Showcase live content from Instagram, Twitter, Facebook, or YouTube using plugins like:

- **Smash Balloon Social Photo Feed:** Displays Instagram photos.
- **Custom Twitter Feeds:** Shows tweets with styling options.
- **Feed Them Social:** Supports multiple social platforms in one plugin.

Social feeds encourage visitors to follow you and stay updated.

Automating Social Media Posting

Tools like **Buffer**, **Hootsuite**, or **Jetpack Publicize** automatically share your new posts to social channels, saving time and increasing consistency.

Building Your Brand Voice

Social media allows direct communication with your audience. Share behind-the-scenes, respond to messages, and build trust by showing authenticity.

Scaling Your Site: From Hobby to Business

Recognizing When to Scale

Your site might start as a passion project but with steady traffic and growing engagement, it's time to think bigger. Signs you're ready include:

- Increasing visitor numbers.
- Growing email lists or memberships.
- Consistent revenue streams.
- Demand for more content, products, or services.

Steps to Scale Successfully

1. **Upgrade Hosting:** Move to managed WordPress hosting for better speed, security, and support.

2. **Invest in Premium Themes and Plugins:** Enhance functionality and design with professional tools.

3. **Hire Help:** Consider freelancers or agencies for content creation, marketing, or technical support.

4. **Expand Content Offerings:** Add courses, ebooks, webinars, or physical products.

5. **Enhance SEO and Marketing:** Implement advanced SEO strategies and paid advertising campaigns.

6. **Build Partnerships:** Collaborate with influencers, affiliates, or complementary businesses.

Monitoring Growth Metrics

Use Google Analytics and other tools to track:

- Traffic sources and patterns.
- Conversion rates.
- Revenue and customer retention.
- User behavior and engagement.

Data-driven decisions help you focus resources efficiently.

Preparing for Long-Term Success

- Regularly review and update your business plan.
- Stay informed on WordPress updates and digital marketing trends.
- Foster your community with ongoing engagement and quality content.

Maintaining and expanding your WordPress site is a journey of ongoing learning and adaptation. By treating comments intelligently, using the power of social media, and scaling effectively, you establish not just a website, but an enduring online presence and business.

Resources for Continuous Learning: Forums, Tutorials, and WordPress Events

Engaging with WordPress Forums

WordPress forums are treasure troves of knowledge and support, offering real-time assistance, expert advice, and peer collaboration.

- **Official WordPress Support Forum:** The first stop for most users, this forum covers a broad range of topics from basic setup to advanced troubleshooting.

- **Stack Exchange - WordPress Development:** Ideal for developers and users seeking technical answers with detailed explanations.

- **Reddit – r/WordPress:** A vibrant community sharing tips, news, and experiences.

- **Facebook Groups and Slack Channels:** Numerous dedicated groups provide niche support and networking opportunities.

Tips for Using Forums Effectively:

- Search before posting questions to avoid duplicates.
- Provide clear, detailed descriptions of your issues.
- Participate actively to learn and contribute.

Mastering Tutorials and Online Courses

Tutorials offer structured learning paths to develop specific skills.

- **WordPress Codex and Developer Resources:** The official documentation is comprehensive and updated regularly.

- **YouTube Channels:** Creators like WPBeginner and WPCrafter offer beginner-friendly video guides.

- **Online Learning Platforms:** Sites like Udemy, LinkedIn Learning, and Coursera provide in-depth WordPress courses covering everything from basics to plugin development.

- **Blogs and Articles:** Follow popular blogs such as WPTavern, Torque, and Smashing Magazine for news, tips, and best practices.

Learning Strategy:

- Combine video tutorials with hands-on practice.
- Take notes and apply new knowledge immediately.
- Join webinars or live workshops to ask questions.

Participating in WordPress Events and Meetups

WordPress community events are excellent for networking, learning, and inspiration.

- **WordCamps:** Informal, community-organized conferences held worldwide focusing on WordPress topics.

- **Meetups:** Smaller, local gatherings where users share knowledge, solve problems, and collaborate.

- **Online Events:** Virtual conferences, workshops, and live Q&A sessions are increasingly popular.

Benefits of Attending Events:

- Direct access to WordPress experts.
- Exposure to new tools and trends.
- Motivation and accountability to advance your skills.

Final Checklist and Troubleshooting Guide for Beginners

Essential Maintenance Checklist

Maintaining your WordPress site requires regular attention to several critical areas. Use this checklist to keep your site healthy and optimized:

- **Backups:** Ensure backups are running regularly and stored safely off-site.
- **Updates:** Keep WordPress core, themes, and plugins updated.
- **Security:** Monitor for suspicious activity, enforce strong passwords, and use security plugins.
- **Performance:** Test site speed, optimize images, and review caching settings.
- **Content:** Review and refresh content for accuracy and relevance.
- **SEO:** Check meta titles, descriptions, and sitemap status.
- **Comments:** Moderate comments and remove spam.
- **Analytics:** Review traffic data and adjust strategies.

Common Issues and How to Troubleshoot Them

Even with proper maintenance, issues may arise. Here are frequent problems and practical solutions:

- **White Screen of Death:**
  Usually caused by plugin or theme conflicts.
  Solution: Deactivate all plugins via FTP and reactivate one by one.

- **Login Issues:**
  Forgotten password or redirect loops.
  Solution: Reset passwords via phpMyAdmin or disable plugins causing conflicts.

- **Slow Website:**
  Caused by unoptimized images, too many plugins, or poor hosting.
  Solution: Optimize media, limit plugins, and consider upgrading hosting.

- **Broken Links and Missing Images:**
  Often result of URL changes or deleted files.

Solution: Use plugins like Broken Link Checker to find and fix.

- **Plugin or Theme Update Fails:**
  Due to server timeouts or permissions.
  Solution: Update manually via FTP or check hosting settings.

When to Seek Professional Help

If problems persist or are beyond your comfort zone:

- Contact your hosting provider for server-related issues.
- Hire WordPress developers or maintenance services for complex fixes.
- Engage with the community forums to get expert recommendations.

Maintaining and expanding your WordPress website is a continual effort powered by learning, diligence, and community support. Leveraging forums, courses, and events gives you fresh knowledge and solutions.

Meanwhile, employing a methodical checklist and troubleshooting guide empowers you to keep your site reliable and performant.

In 2025, success consists in dedication to growth and adaptation. Your WordPress adventure is ongoing—embrace it with confidence and curiosity.

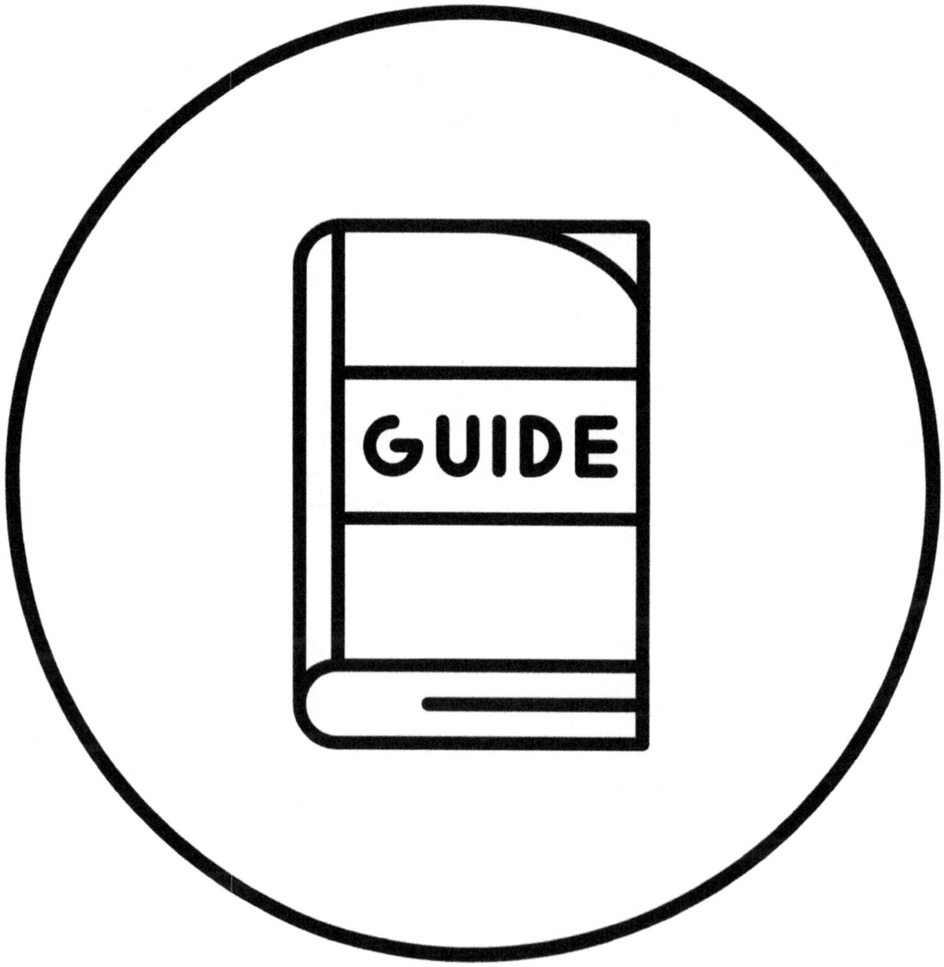
GUIDE

Conclusion

Congratulations. By reaching this point, you have taken a crucial step toward understanding one of the most effective tools for developing your internet presence.

WordPress is more than just software—it is a gateway to sharing your ideas, establishing your brand, launching a business, or building a community that cares.

The landscape of the web is always evolving. New updates, difficulties, and possibilities come every day. But the foundation you've developed through this guide empowers you not merely to face such changes but to utilize them in your favor.

Remember, success with WordPress is not about perfection on day one—it is about consistency, learning, and adaptation.

Use the skills and information you've gained to experiment fearlessly, connect authentically with your audience, and design a website that reflects your vision and ambition.

> **Your Wordpress Journey Is Just Beginning. Stay Curious. Stay Dedicated. And Keep Developing. The Web Is Waiting For What Only You Can Build.**

Printed in Dunstable, United Kingdom